IT'S YOUR BUSINESS

It's YOUR Business

Authors and Creative Businessowners

LYNDA REES

Sweetwater Publishing Company

It's YOUR Business
For Authors and Creative Businessowners
By
Lynda Rees
The Murder Guru
Love is a dangerous mystery.
Enjoy the ride!©

LyndaReesAuthor.com
LyndaReesAuthor@gmail.com

It's YOUR Business
For Authors and Creative Businessowners
By Lynda Rees, The Murder Guru

Email: lyndareesauthor@gmail.com
Website: http://www.lyndareesauthor.com
Original Edition
ISBN:PRINT 978-1-960763-00-6
ISBN Ebook:978-1-960763-03-7
Copyright © 2024 by Publisher:
Sweetwater Publishing Company
6612 Ky. Hwy. 17 North, DeMossville, KY 41033
http://www.sweetwaterpublishingcompany.wordpress.com

TABLE OF CONTENTS:

This course will cover the following:
TITLE PAGE
COPYWRITE PAGE
RIGHTS RESERVED
#1 INTRODUCTION
#2 OVERVIEW
#3 BRANDING
#4 STAYING LEGAL

· Keeping Records – The IRS and Finances (Tool/Handout)
· Copywriting Overview
· Eternal Book Rights

#5 BUSINESS PLANNING
#6 GROWTH

· Networking and Writer Organizations (Handout)
· Education Resources for Writers

#7 KEEP IT STRAIGHT

REMEMBER THE 4 P SYSTEM

PROACTIVE – PROFESSIONAL –
POSITIVE - PERSISTENT

CHAPTER ONE
INTRODUCTION

Since you're reading this, it's safe to assume you are involved in some sort of creative business that requires you to provide your form of art to the public for a charge. Whatever form of creative work you do, whether it's writing books, poetry, short stories, painting, photography, design, acting, producing movies, narrating, voice acting, crafting, or anything else you do that creates a work of art you intend to sell to the public, this book will hold value for you.

I am Lynda Rees, The Murder Guru. My tag line is "Love is a dangerous mystery. Enjoy the ride!©" So, why am I an expert at business practices? Let me explain that.

Before I became a full-time author, I worked for over thirty-six-years in corporate America for Procter &Gamble, a Fortune 500 Company. My careers there were in Marketing and Global Transportation and Logistics. I managed $50+-million-dollar budgets, negotiated ocean freight for the company's international business and did marketing for several brands I'm sure you'll recognize—Comet®, Spic 'N Span®, Mr. Clean®, and Swiffer®, I also managed marketing operations for some of their top five US customers.

During this career, I wrote training and qualification manuals and taught customer service representatives and trainers. I wrote business proposals, marketing plans, presentations, sales, and training manuals, did copywriting, developed advertising materials, worked on television commercials and other media ads, and wrote contracts. I negotiated ocean freight rates for the company's international shipping and worked with worldwide contacts, heads of the largest shipping companies in the world, and government and customs officials. This required me to travel extensively in Asia, South and Central America, and the Caribbean and to absorb the culture and customs of many counties as I interacted with international internal and external business associates.

My dual career was in financial investments and real estate. As V. P. of a financial services group, I held licenses with the Security and Exchange Commission. I trained and managed a large sales force that assisted individuals and small businesses to establish retirement plans. We sold securities, insurance, and mortgages.

For thirty-four years, I was a residential agent for the largest real estate company in the Greater Cincinnati Area. In this role, I helped people achieve their dreams of homeownership, negotiated deals, wrote listing and sales contracts, and assisted buyers to obtain mortgages in the ever-changing world of finance.

My love has always been fiction, so I continued to write what I enjoy without seeking publication. As I contemplated leaving the corporate world, my journey to become a fiction author became a reality.

My first two books were published simultaneously, one with a publisher and the other as an Indi-author. Both of my debut novels won accolades from RWA's RITA and PFTHRW contests. Gold Lust Conspiracy is my award-winning historical romance. Parsley, Sage, Rose, Mary & Wine is Book 1 of The Bloodline Series, a spicy romantic mystery.

At the time of this book's publication, I've gone on to publish ten books in The Bloodline Series, three in the trilogy The Reggie Chronicles, eight stand-alone mysteries, one historical romance, four children's stories, and several non-fiction and self-help books.

I have found that most authors are versed and focused on the creative aspect of writing. This only makes sense. We get into the literary business because we want to share our stories with the world, whether they be novels or non-fiction. Once those stories are created, however, we need to make them available to the public.

Regardless of which road we take to market, we—the writers now become businesspeople. To do this, we must choose a publishing route. We may partner with a publisher or not, but it is our responsibility to guide the process and manage our careers as authors. No one is going to care about your creative work and your career more than you do.

It is time to take off our creative hat and put on our management that. You, as the author, are now the CEO of your company. You must now think of your book from a totally different perspective.

This requires a completely different mindset. There are many things to consider.

First of all, you must now think of your book as a product. It is an item you wish to position properly in the marketplace, at the right price, in the correct locations, so your target audience will find it and purchase it.

You love your book. Right? You want readers to love it. No doubt.

Who wants to read it?

Why? What makes it special?

What monetary value does it have?

What is it going to cost to publish it?

What will it take to market it?

How do you find readers who will want to purchase it?

How will you make them aware your book exists?

How do you attract them once you find them?

How do you get it on shelves in bookstores, libraries, and online?

What is the perfect price point for your work?

This list goes on and on. It can be overwhelming. Don't be baffled by it. I'm going to demystify much of that in this book.

I hope you enjoy the read and find at least one thing that helps make your author business experience easier and more profitable.

I have created the 4P System. That is:

1. Be Proactive
2. Be Professional
3. Be Positive
4. Be Persistent

So, let's get started.

REMEMBER THE 4 P SYSTEM

PROACTIVE – PROFESSIONAL –
POSITIVE - PERSISTENT

CHAPTER TWO
OVERVIEW

You are completing a book and ready to publish it. Now what do you do with it?

That depends on what your goals are. If writing is a hobby for you and you don't care if anyone reads it, put this book down. It's not for you.

If your vision is to become a successful author with lots of people reading your book, you need to manage your writing life as a real business.

Success isn't easy. If it were, everyone would be successful. It's hard work. It takes time and energy. There is a learning curve, regardless of where you start from. So, if your goal is success, you must devote your most valuable resources to it.

What are they?

Time and energy.

Carve out come of these valuable resources for yourself and your author business. Devote time and your energy to learning a bit about how the industry, your craft, and how to manage your business. The latter is what we're focusing on in this book.

I'm going to share business tips and tricks I've learned over my many years in business that I've applied to my writing career. I'm also sharing much of what I've learned along my author journey, to help make yours as stress-free as possible adventure.

I've developed tools and am providing them to you. Use them to help move your business forward.

Taking charge of your enterprise isn't complex, but there is a learning curve. Hopefully, this class will shorten your learning curve.

It's time for you to take your author hat off. Don your CEO hat. You are the owner of your company.

PLANNING:

Two templates are included in your package. One is for creating a Business Plan. Any business should have an overall plan of who they are, how they operate, what they provide and to whom they intend to provide that. This is for the life of the business, a working document that can be modified as market, industry and your plans change. It should specify what you want to do for the first year, year two, year five and project to year ten.

The second is a template to help you plan how you're going to achieve the Business Plan. This one is for an Action Plan. This is a working document you will use each year to move one year closer to the overall ten-year plan. It should list what 4-5 goals you want to achieve-GOAL, how you intend to do that—STRATEGY, what you will do to achieve each strategy—TACTICS (the work), and by what deadline you will achieve each strategy—TIMELINE.

A goal is no good to you without a timeline. The timeline is a date by which you can measure progress. We get good at what we measure.

REMEMBER THE 4 P SYSTEM

PROACTIVE – PROFESSIONAL – POSITIVE - PERSISTENT

CHAPTER THREE
BRANDING

You are your Brand. What does that mean? In this chapter I will share some branding and strategy insights.

WHAT? A brand is the look and feel, the personality of your business. It clearly shows the audience, at a glance, who you are and what you represent. It is your face to the public—the one you want to put out for them to see and recognize.

WHY? Brand identity should resonate with your target audience. It should speak directly to those people you want to reach with your message and products. It should be clear and consistent.

By adopting fundamental elements of the branding process, you can create a branding instrument that should provide continuous growth and a competitive advantage.

A brand is a real, tangible tool with measurable impact on your business. Therefore, it is crucial to be strategic.

The Harvard Business Review article penned by American Entrepreneur Dan Pallotta, succinctly captures the heart of branding: *"Brand is everything, and everything is brand."*

In today's world, buyers are empowered to make informed purchasing decisions. Therefore, you must earn their business. This makes branding more and more important for business growth.

A strong brand will help convince people to buy more, pay higher prices and decide quicker to purchase your product. It will also help buyers become loyal purchasers to the point where they become advocates for your products.

Using strong branding in your marketing efforts will help make it more efficient and help you stay competitive in the industry. Using key strategic benefit messaging and strong branding can drive motivation to purchase and alleviate buyer concerns about product pricing. This allows you to set premium pricing on your products.

HOW?

MISSION, VISION, AND VALUE

Don't make the common mistake of talking about the things **you** value. Frame your value statement as actionable behaviors.

Your vision should describe where you're going.

Your mission explains why.

Your values describe how you are going to behave along the way.

For example:

Mission

I want to lie in the sun on a rock on top of the tallest mountain in the U.S.A.

Vision

I will hike to the top of this mountain.

Values

I will climb safely and slowly. I will help other climbers I meet along the path.

Values help you decide how to behave. They are critical to creating a culture and should become a meaningful part of your day-to-day work life.

From your Mission Vision and Values, you can create an overall statement of who you are and what you are bringing to the world. I have provided a tool to help you plan your work life based on these this overall statement. It is a working document that can be evaluated as the year progresses, so you can step up where you need to and scale back if necessary.

Using this tool, you will define three-to-five Goals you wish to achieve for the year to support your overall statement and get you to the place you want to be within your long-term plan.

Fill this template in each year with these items. The Goal Setting Tool handout will explain how you do that.

Within each Goal, what Strategies will help you reach that particular Goal? Within each Strategy, what Tactics do you need to use to achieve the Strategy? By what date do you need to accomplish each Tactic? This last section of the tool may be the most important. It provides motivation to achieve the work by a specific date.

That also helps you a measurement by which you can evaluate how well you did at the end of the year. Each year, review the overall statement at the top of the template. Review how you achieved each goal. Don't beat yourself up if you didn't accomplish everything you wanted to. It's good to have stretching goals. Simply determine how to work the remainder of that achievement into next year's plan. Or decide it was fine as you left. Also, you could determine it is not necessary to achieve in order to reach your Goal. As I mentioned previously, this tool is a working document subject to change as needed.

CONSISTENCY

Consistent, strong branding can help your products thrive regardless of challenging dynamics in the marketplace. What type of challenges? There are many. Among them are slow market growth, lower profit margins, inflation causing rising production costs and less buyer spending.

With strategic branding you have an opportunity to meet or exceed your objective, regardless of market conditions. Your Brand Strategy Drives Business Growth and directly affects the buyer's willingness to pay for your product. It is all about perception.

The value of perception is measurable when it comes to pricing. If two authors sell nearly identical products, the one with stronger branding will be able to achieve sales or possibly elevate the price point. Buyer willingness to purchase is inspired by your branding.

If a buyer selects a similar brand to yours, the fundamental reason is not the product's price point. The weaker the brand, the harder it is to achieve a sale regardless of price. The lower the price, the more questions it raises in a buyers' mind about the quality and value of your product.

The intrinsic value of your product is set by your brand's ability to consistently relate to the buyer—what they need or desire—not what you care about.

Yes, you must communicate the benefits of your product, but the core message should be about why it matters to the buyer or what's in it for them. Why do they care?

Position your brand messaging focusing on the buyers' interests. This allows you to build substantial equity in their minds that you have a better product.

Brand equity is important, but you must get the message out. Awareness is key. Marketing and public relations are vital to success. You must reach the right parties and provide newsworthy industry achievements and/or third-party referrals. We will dig into marketing and public relations more in a later chapter.

BUYING PROCESS

As a seller of your product, you need to understand who your readers are and how they make buying decisions. Buyers go through three-stages as they make purchasing decisions.

- They must trust they're buying a worthy product.
- They want a product with credibility.
- By providing answers to potential objections, you can shorten a buyer's decision cycle and get to the purchase point quicker.
- Two things are key—awareness and quality.

As I said earlier, a strong brand is designed to convince buyers to purchase more, pay higher prices, make quicker buying decisions, remain loyal to your brand, and become advocates for your products.

Branding is about improving buyer perception. It also makes the product itself more valuable. As you develop your brand, evaluate the customer's journey to purchase. Study the touch points in that journey.

- What steps to they take to get to the sale?
- What do they consider before buying?
- What are they concerned about?
- What do they want?
- How do they go about finding it? Where do they look?
- Once they get there, how do they evaluate the selection available?
- Why would they choose yours over similar offerings?

Now, to improve sales of your product, you must create customer awareness at these touch points. Keep in mind, people will pay more for a brand they trust and love.

BRAND CONSISTENCY

To achieve success, your business must run on a proven process. You must maintain organization and you must optimize and repetitively repeat that process.

One FREE element you can achieve will boost your product's value. That is brand consistency. I said it before, but it bears repeating. Consistency in product increases overall value by reinforcing your position in the market. This can help attract quality buyers, maintain higher retention rates of readership, and raise the perception value of your products.

On the contrary, if your message and look are inconsistent, erratic buyers will be confused and mistrust you. This will be reflected in slower-to-buy decisions, lower sales, and loss of readership to reduction in trust that you will deliver what they want from you.

A consistent brand helps you begin to take ownership of your specific niche in the marketplace. Taking a position makes it more difficult for a competitor to steal your marketplace advantage. Consistency trains buyers on what to expect from you. Reinforcing your brand continually sets expectations and builds a foundation for continued success.

Consistency helps customers come along for the journey when you launch a new product. They see this as the next step in their experience with you and your product and makes them more likely to purchase new offerings.

COMPONENTS

Your brand is your identity. It's what your customer knows you by, who you are to them. What do you want them to know about you?

Branding includes several components. Among the basic building blocks of a consistent brand are messaging, tone, visual image, and delivery. These four things impact your brand. Let's get deeper into each of them.

Message

A consistent brand message should define your position. Who are you? What do you provide? Do you write mystery and suspense? Do you write horror? Fantasy? Are you a narrator or a voice actor?

Your message should support your core behaviors. Your actions must be consistent with your message so customers will trust and be happy with what you deliver. It will prevent buyer disappointment or the feeling they've been cheated. It will draw the right customers to your product.

Tone

Tone helps communicate what buyers can expect from you. It is about look, feel and sound. If you write horror stories, pastel colors, hearts, and rainbows in your messaging will confuse the reader. If you write children's books, don't use sexy models on your book covers. Tone explains to the buyer what feeling or experience they will get from your book. It sets an expectation of what their journey with your book will be like. Don't sell the item. Sell the experience the buyer will get from your product.

Design

Imagery is key to your brand consistency toolkit. Use visuals thoughtfully and strategically to increase customer recognition. You want them to know immediately upon a glance that this is your book.

Design includes elements like color, font, visuals. If you write sweet romance, don't put naked people on your cover. If you write contemporary romance, don't put gothic dressed models on the cover. If you write comedy, don't put monsters there, unless the story is about a hysterically funny monster. You get the drift.

Here's an example of great branding from one of my favorite authors, Janet Evanovich, of how to show consistency on a cover.

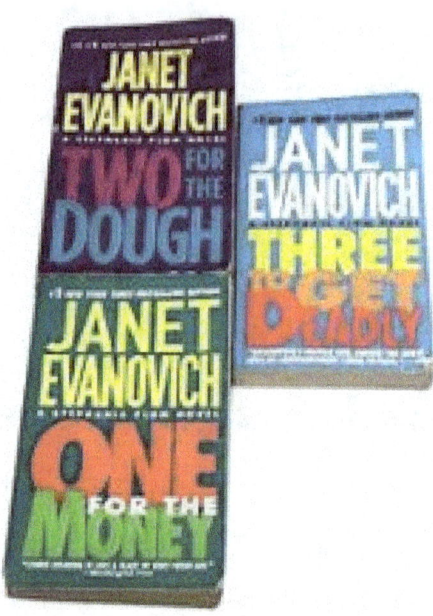

You can see how she consistently uses font and color throughout the Stephanie Plum series. This use of look and feel allows fans to recognize her identity immediately when they see the cover.

One distinction, however, is that over the many years as she wrote these and several standalone books, her name became more important than the title of the book. She shifted the balance of font size in order to benefit from her growing popularity.

Here's an example from another of my favorite authors, Jana DeLeon. Note the use of color, imagery, font, placement of title, and author name. These attributes contribute to the overall look, feel, and design of the cover. You can tell immediately that she writes mystery, comedy, and, set in the bayou, and that it the stories are written by Jana DeLeon. You can tell from her covers what she will deliver.

Consistency builds increasing legal protection for your brand should a competitor attempt to copy or imitate it. By consistently using the same brand identity, you establish your legal ownership of it. For instance, my pen name and author tag are below. I use this on any communication I publish to the world. Applying it continually proves legally that I own this name and tag. It also communicates that I write murder mysteries with a bit of romance. Since most of my books are set in Kentucky horse country, "the ride" signifies the setting.

Lynda Rees, The Murder Guru
Love is a dangerous mystery. Enjoy the ride!©

Delivery

Using your brand throughout time and across all channels

contributes to consistency of the buying experience. Channels you choose to communicate with buyers through, as well as frequency of contact, create a rhythm of communication. The effectiveness of this contact increases as time passes, as you become a familiar face to the public. It results in the readership learning to better understand you through continual contact and the type of communication you have with them. Readers learn to depend on you to provide them with quality.

Take the time to learn what your audience perceives of you. Periodically listen to your buyers and hear what they believe to be your brand promise. You might consider doing a customer survey or poll to garner valuable information and insight. Establish loops of communication so you can track your reader's satisfaction and glean insight on to how you might better provide what your readers want from you. When you know what they're thinking and believe about your products, you can transform weaknesses into advantages.

Scale

Be consistent and provide concentrated effort over time. Set goals and create a scalable plan.

Start small. Begin with personal conversations with readers through social media or a newsletter. Test your strategy as you go and adjust as needed.

Measure responsiveness to your message. What is working? What is not? Does it need improving, or should you drop efforts that are not successful?

Do more of what works and less of what is not. Focus on what is working. Increase successful tactics.

Periodically check in to ensure you are on the right track. Monitor perception and measure efforts. Then scale your efforts toward those that provide sales and growth. Stay aligned to your business strategy.

Strengthen Your Message

Regardless of what methods you choose to use to reach your readership, be aware of the experience you provide them with and leverage it. Personally, I use social media, my website, and newsletter to stay in touch with readers and to attract new readership.

What touch points do you have with them? Be intentional about how you use your fan base. Be consistent and stay on target for the greater mission by tying communication to your core values so readers understand how your brand attributes directly affect what matters to them.

Be responsive and available to loyal readers. Show you value them. Give them something extra, a reward for loyalty. This can be something as simple as recognition, bonus reads, freebees, swag, first-to-read chapters, extra chapters, etc.

Look for opportunities to create positive associations. Is it on-strategy to align yourself or a book you've published with an organization for a partnership or endorsement? Don't miss an opportunity to focus support on causes that represent your goals and values. Alignment with the right source can be very powerful and increase your value in the eyes of your target audience.

This could be a charity organization. Or it could be an educational or research institution. There should be benefits to both you and them. An organization's attributes could support your brand and/or book in turn, providing advantages for both you and them. You both benefit from the added exposure.

As your brand grows and you maintain consistency, management of this requires less effort. Readers become familiar with your name and books and how your communication is displayed across different channels and touchpoints. This awareness is a valuable asset that directly affects the cost and resources required to maintain exposure. Investment becomes minimal compared to overall business returns.

REMEMBER THE 4 P SYSTEM

PROACTIVE – PROFESSIONAL – POSITIVE – PERSISTENT

CHAPTER FOUR
STAY LEGAL

How does one stay legal?

RECORDS, IRS, FINANCE, RIGHTS (See Handout Page)

For the IRS and publishing industry to take you seriously, you must act as the business owner. You are now not only a writer or published author. You are the CEO of your company.

You must operate as such in order to stay legal, out of trouble with the IRS, to make the most of your writing business, and to spread the word that your book is out there for everyone to read.

In this lesson, I will explain how to keep immaculate records for your business and for your writing process. I'll explain how to establish your business. How to find professionals to network with and learn from your peers. How to manage finances and the basics of copywriting.

The IRS expects you to keep flawless records of expenditures. You will find yourself spending cash to find the right agent or publisher, hire an editor if you are self-publishing, join organizations like Derby Rotten Scoundrels, Romance Writers of America, Sisters in Crime, Mystery Writers of America, or any of the hundreds of professional writing organizations. These groups are of great value to you as a business owner, to network and learn from your peers, attend classes to study craft and the every-changing industry.

You may need to hire a publicist, place ads to promote your book, purchase a book cover, hire a virtual or in-person assistant, purchase research material, or travel. The list is endless. There is a multitude of items you will spend money on to write and promote your business. How does that work?

Whether it's income or money spent, you must keep organized records to protect yourself and your work. You must prove your intention of making a profit—at some point.

At first there might be more outflow than inflow, but if you're managing the enterprise in a professional manner, it can be taken seriously as a company. Until you are clearing a profit, money spent could be considered personal loan to your proven business venture from you as the lender. As always, check with your tax expert. I am NOT an accountant, simply an author sharing what I've learned. A professional accountant should be expert in tax laws as they pertain to small businesses and the ever-changing IRS laws.

Many things you spend money on can possibly qualify as tax deductions. For instance, mileage to and from business events, your home office, computer, wi-fi, and supplies, membership fees for professional organizations, etc., could be considered deductions. This is true, but only the percentage used toward your professional venture and only if you keep clear, accurate records of spending.

Once you are making considerable profit from book sales, you might want to check with your entertainment attorney to determine if you should establish a corporation. There can be security and possibly financial benefits of incorporation that could protect you and your income. This is something that should be considered on an individual business, as they are not all alike; and it can be a personal preference.

I am not a lawyer. I don't advise for or against this. It may be worth looking into. I simply wanted to make you aware the opportunity is available to you as a professional author.

The spreadsheet handout I am providing you shows how I track spending. This method ensures that when the time comes to file tax reports, I have accurate records.

I establish a worksheet on this workbook for each year. As I spend money, I add to the spreadsheet the total spent for that item and an explanation and date of the expenditure. This covers everything I need to track, but if you have something special, you can always add another set of columns for that specific category.

The spreadsheet includes formulas, so columns add up at the bottom. Once this year is over, I print this out and provide it along with receipts for the items on the spreadsheet, to my accountant. This allows him to manage my filings.

To move to the next year, I simply create another tab and move to the next worksheet inside the workbook—the one for the new year to start the new year's summary of expenses.

It is necessary to keep receipts in order to back up expenses filed in tax reporting. This means you must keep electronic and/or paper copies. If you are ever audited, the IRS will require you to produce these records. You can pull them from your paper files or print them if they are electronic. Ask your accountant how long you must keep them, as tax laws are subject to change.

I keep one file drawer specifically for receipts of the current year's expenses. Inside that drawer are color-coded folders for each item I expect to collect receipts for during the year (e.g.: Ads, Misc. Expenses, Events, Publication, Organizations, etc.). This allows me to quickly find what I need in my physical file drawer.

There I keep hard copies of receipts, because not everything I spend money on is done electronically. I do, however, have identical file folders on my computer (or cloud) where I keep copies of electronic receipts for simplicity. I print all receipts as hard copies, so I will never have to go back to previous years to find electronic files. That way at the end of the year, I simply scan the online folders to ensure I didn't forget to print something.

When tax time rolls around, I pull out each physical folder and remove receipts for the year. I double check them against what's on the spreadsheet to ensure I didn't forget to log something.

Once all receipts are logged in, I print the spreadsheet and provide that along with any tax papers I've received (1040, 1098, Mortgage Tax papers, etc.), anything that is required to be attached when taxes are filed. I give this large packet of spreadsheet information along with all my personal documents to my accountant.

Not only will he want business details, but he also needs personal tax information. In addition to my business spreadsheet, I provide a spreadsheet that includes the cost for running my household. He will determine what of that he can use toward deductions.

Why? As a professional author, I'm running a business from my home office. This means my workspace in the house and business expenses like a portion of wi-fi, computer, etc., are business expenses. By providing my accountant with a list of household yearly expenses, like heat, electricity, wi-fi, water, sanitation, insurance, and mortgage cost, he can calculate what portion should be attributed to the running of my company. This is a mathematical equation I'm not interested in learning. For me, it's well worth paying a professional to handle it.

The same is true of your automobile. You should keep a log of mileage driven for business in your vehicle. You can also keep gas receipts for dollars spent on business travel. You can't deduct both. So, it makes sense to use whichever one provides the greater tax deduction.

Your accountant can help you with this decision. At first you might consider doing it both ways, until you can determine which is most effective for your specific vehicle usage. Either way, you are expected to keep accurate records. Don't wait until the end of the year and try to recreate it. It's much easier to keep an accurate log as you go. Simply put a dedicated notepad in your vehicle for this purpose.

I don't want to manage or even know all of the mind-blowing complexities of tax calculations for authors. I'm happy to have a professional take care of my taxes, so I can concentrate on writing and managing my business. I've found my accountant well worth the money spent on him to administer tax filings for me.

When I'm finished with them, I put business receipts into a box or large envelope for storing this year's taxes. Receipts should be kept for seven years (Check with your tax expert on this timing, as it's subject to change.). When my taxes are filed, I put my copy in this box and store it where I keep such long-term records.

COPYRIGHT OVERVIEW—PROTECTING YOUR WORK

Once you create a work, you own it. It is automatically copyrighted.

If you have a tag, logo, or something you want to own, you must show consistent use of it, to make it yours. Consistent use of it shows ownership.

There is no requirement to file an official copywrite with the government for this or for your books. There is, however, the opportunity. Doing that could have potential benefits for you, should an entity try to steal your work.

When is my work protected?

Your work is under copyright protection the moment it is created and fixed in a tangible form that it is perceptible either directly or with the aid of a machine or device.

Do I have to register with your office to be protected?

No. In general, registration is voluntary. Copyright exists from the moment the work is created. You will have to register, however, if you wish to bring a lawsuit for infringement of a U.S. work. See Circular 1, Copyright Basics, section "Copyright Registration."

I'm not an attorney but have obtained advice from intellectual attorneys in the past. Filing an official copywrite protects your work should it be stolen, and you need to file a legal claim and take the party to court.

The copywrite must be filed prior to the theft, in this case. Once something is stolen, it's difficult to sue the guilty party. Not impossible. Difficult. If your work is officially filed with the Copyright office when you create it—before it is stolen—you have a much easier way of obtaining monetary compensation for loss or damage to your work.

Why should I register my work if copyright protection is automatic?

Registration is recommended for a number of reasons. Many choose to register their works because they wish to have the facts of their copyright on the public record and have a certificate of registration. Registered works may be eligible for statutory damages and attorney's fees in successful litigation.

Finally, if registration occurs within five years of publication, it is considered prima facie evidence in a court of law. See Circular 1, Copyright Basics, section "Copyright Registration" and Circular 38b, Highlights of Copyright Amendments Contained in the Uruguay Round Agreements Act (URAA), on non-U.S. works.

The process of filing a copyright is complex and can be costly, but it is doable. It must be filed separately for each version (eBook, print, hardcopy, audio, etc.), and there's a new charge for each version. I've done it with my work.

If you work with a publisher, they will likely file the copyright. Be sure this is detailed in your contract with them, and that it states they are filing the copyright in your name—not theirs.

You can register your copyright at the following address."

You will have to register if you wish to bring a lawsuit for infringement of a U.S. work."

Copyright office website: https://www.copyright.gov/help/faq/index.html

Technically, a "book is copyrighted the moment it is created and fixed in a tangible form that it is perceptible either directly or with the aid of a machine or device," This is a quote from the U. S. Copywrite Office. You don't have to do anything specific (unlike patents, which we will not go into).

PUBLIC DOMAIN

How long do you and your heirs have the rights to your books before they become part of the Public Domain? This is when anyone can secure the book and publish it. A book enters Public Domain as these things occur:

- It was published before 1923.
- It was published before Jan. 1, 1964, and it was not renewed in the 28th year after publication.
- The copyright has expired.
- The copyright owner failed to follow copyright renewal rules.
- The copyright owner deliberately places it in the public domain, known as "dedication." Copyright law does not protect this type of work.

ETERNAL BOOK RIGHT

In the event of death rights to intellectual property goes to the deceased's heir, including financial benefits from the work.

Your work is considered intellectual property, a tangible asset that can be handed down as part of your estate to your beneficiaries upon death. They can continue to publish the work and receive royalties on it. You may want to consult a financial planning or estate planning attorney to learn how to protect your estate for future generations.

ESTATE PLANNING

My advice for estate planning is to be proactive. Do not leave things dangling for heirs to clean up. A financial mess or lack of planning on your part could result in a rift that could break up relationships with family and other heirs. Don't do this to your loved ones. Ensure your final wishes are followed.

Estate planning is not complex, but it is advisable to consult a professional estate planning attorney. Sit down and talk with them about your assets, debts, your final wishes, and how you want those things handled.

Your attorney should be able to prepare a few documents that clearly state those things, so there is no confusion with the probate court, IRS, or among those destined to inherit your estate. It becomes a simple matter to execute your estate plan.

WILL: This can be a simple or as complex a document as you choose, but it should clearly state what disposition should take place of your assets once your debts and final expenses have been covered.

DURABLE POWER OF ATTORNEY: This document establishes who should:

- Take possession, manage, receive money for sales of property or cash paid to you.
- Pay your final debts and expenses, including their Attorney-In-Fact expenses, Deposit funds, make withdrawals from, or sign checks or drafts against your account in your name.
- Pay debts and expenses.
- Retain investments, invest, and reinvest stocks, bonds, securities, or any kind of real personal property.

- Vote, give proxies, exercise rights of conversion for securities, deposit shares, transfer them, or in general, manage your shares and securities.
- Manage real estate, including sell, lease, develop, maintain.
- Take control and operate your business
- Purchase or maintain policies needed to manage the estate.
- Borrow money in your name and/or take necessary action to collect money or property due to you.
- Execute and deliver in your name contracts, deeds, mortgages, leases, security agreements, receipts, releases, returns, reports, and any other document needed to manage the estate.
- Prepare and file tax returns.
- Transfer or convey all assets and act as trustee for any Trust established by you.
- Execute and deliver instruments of release waver renunciation or disclaimer required by law to satisfy legal requirements.
- Make annual gifts to children, grandchildren, great grandchildren and their spouses of tax free per donee amounts such as gifts.
- Exercise stock option grants, write, purchase, sell calls, options and rights held by you.
- Have full investment power over profit sharing plans, pensions, 401K, IRA and other retirement plans.

LIVING WILL: This document states what competent adult person you wish to have power of attorney to exercise your health care needs, should you be unable to do so for yourself.

It should state what powers they can and cannot refuse, how life-sustaining treatment should be handled or withdrawn when you are suffering from an irreversible, incurable, unbearable condition caused by disease, illness, or injury where death is imminent within a very short time.

It should clarify how your health treatment should be handled should you be in permanent unconsciousness characterized by irreversible unawareness of yourself and your environment due to cerebral cortical functioning, resulting in you having no capacity to experience pain or suffering, or your attending physician determines to a reasonable degree of medical certainty there is no reasonable possibility you will regain capacity to make informed health care decisions yourself.

It should explain if they can or cannot withdraw health care needed to provide comfort care.

The document should state how a pregnancy situation should be handled.

It should state that the person should act consistently with your desires if they are known, and act in your best interest.

LIVING TRUST: This is an extremely important document that can save your family drastic amounts of tax money by holding your assets within a trust and appointing someone to manage that trust on behalf of the trustees acquiring the Living Trust upon your death.

It should name **major asset holdings** that are in the Trust and state how any previously non-identified assets should be transferred upon your death into the trust.

Think of this as a place where your assets are accumulated, held, and managed. This includes all titled assets such as cars, boats, motorcycles, stocks, bonds, mutual funds, partnerships, corporations, real estate, investment accounts, bank accounts, or other assets with a title to prove ownership. It includes all tangible property such as appliances, furniture, coin collections, jewelry, artwork, etc. They can be covered by a "blanket" Assignment of Personal Property, which moves them to become part of the trust. It also includes beneficiary designated assets such as insurance, IRAs, retirement plans, annuities, 401Ks and pensions.

The trust document should **name the person** who is to manage the trust—the Trustee. should name the person responsible for managing the trust and how they should be paid for this administrative work.

Creating this document is not something you should attempt to do on your own. **Hire a professional** to quickly, efficiently, and accurately protect your financial well-being, and those of your heirs. It is well worth the small amount you will pay for these documents, to have peace of mind that your hard-earned property will not be unduly taxed upon your death.

HOMEWORK

Do a search and create a list of local entertainment attorneys in your area.

1. Search local listings for professional accountants.
2. Visit the Copywrite link I provided. Read information there about copywriting and determine if that is a route you are interested in pursuing.

REMEMBER THE 4 P SYSTEM

PROACTIVE – PROFESSIONAL –
POSITIVE - PERSISTENT

CHAPTER FIVE
BUSINESS PLANNING

To be taken seriously in the industry and with financial institutions that might be of assistance to you, a professional approach to your company is important. That is why business planning is so important. You need to understand what your company represents, where it is currently, where you want it to go and by when, and how you intend to get there. Those are the key items of a business plan.

First, let's discuss the writing industry. Regardless of which genre you are involved in, there is data available that can help you determine its value and what the particular niche market you want to obtain for yourself is worth. This is simply an example of how to look at the overall industry you are working in

I am providing some tidbits of data about the romance publishing industry that might explain its value.

- Romance is the most popular genre of books sold.
- $1.44 Billion in revenue for romance books, the highest sales genre.

- If I can sell to .0033, a third of a percent of them, that is $4.752 Million in sales.
- 47-Million Romance books sold/year.
- 29% of my fiction readers prefer Romance.
- 33% of Paperbacks sold are romance books.
- More than 50% of books sold in 2021 were romance books.

(Data according to Penguin Random House.)
So, it is worth it. It also shows me what I can target.
What now?
Defining your target audience will help determine how best to approach them. For instance, I've learned these things about my readership.

In the United States the writing and publishing industry presently looks like this:

- My target audience is 18-64-year-old readers.
    - Within that specifically 18-44 is the largest group.
- 29.6 Million books/year within this age range.
- Those sales amount to $907.2 Million/year.
- 25% of them are 18-29-year-olds. That is $226.8 Million/year.
- 28% are 30–44-year-olds. That's another $254.0 Million/year.
- 17% are 45–54-year-olds.
- 11% are 55-64-year-olds.

By targeting 18–44-year-old readers, I can get the largest bang for my marketing buck, targeting 53% of my possible readership for a piece of that $480.8 Million/year. Even reaching for 1/3 of a percent (not even 1%), of that audience that is a measly $1.59-Million/year.

· My target audience buys books: 24% in store, 18% online.
· 42% of readers in my target market read via tablet.
· 30% read on an eReader.
· 16% read on phones.

That means 72% of my readers either use a tablet or eReader. That means eBooks or audiobooks are what they are seeking. Another 24% of them read physical books. That's 96% of my readers. That means it's worth it to produce all three formats.

Now we know why and who, we need to determine how. Creating a Business Plan helps define that.

So, how do you create one? I've provided an example of how to write one. You can find other templates online for purchase.

By going through this exercise, I have identified that:

· 72% of my readers use a tablet or eReader enjoying eBooks or audiobooks.
· In 72% of my target market revenue is $653.18 Million/year.
· Aiming for 1/3 of a percent (.0033) of that market, potential sales would be $2.16 Million/year with my eBooks and audiobooks, plus paperback or hardback book sales.

CONCLUSION

The market is sufficient to warrant targeting eBook and audiobook sales to romance readers between the ages of 18-44. My secondary target is physical book sales to this age group. This is a clearly defined target.

GOALS/STRATEGIES/TACTICS/MEASUREMENTS

There is a simple way to track and schedule your plan of action. Start with your mission statement.

Then staying in line with that statement, what are the top 3-5 goals you have for the year. Goals are the **WHAT**.

For each goal, what Strategies will you use to achieve them.

Strategies are the **HOW**. How do you intend to pursue these goals?

Next are Tactics. What actions will you take to achieve each of these strategies? Tactics are the **STEPS** you make toward accomplishing the Strategy.

Lastly, there is the timeline. This is the measurement tool or target date by which you wish to complete each Tactic. It's the **WHEN** used in measuring success toward your goals. We get better at things we measure and improve.

Below is a simple chart that will help you track your Goals, Strategies, Tactics and Measurements. If you do this each year, then evaluate it as you go along, you will find you can easily make improvements to the way you manage your business.

PLAN OF ACTION YEAR _____ FOR

_____

MISSION STATEMENT:

GOAL	STRATEGY	TACTIC	MEASUREMENT

SUMMARY

Your Mission Statement is the overall thing you want to achieve. It should be broad, clear, and concise—no more than 2-3 sentences.

Goals are the things you need to accomplish in order to become or do what you mentioned in the mission statement. You should have no more than 3-5 goals for your business.

Strategies for each goal are the ways you intend to go about achieving each goal.

Tactics are specific jobs or things you will do to support the strategies.

Each Tactic should have a Timeline. That is the measurement.

HOMEWORK

1. Research the genre you write in and determine which age group reads books like yours.
2. What formats are they using to read—eBook, audiobook, Print.
3. What is the size of the prize for the genre you write?

REMEMBER THE 4 P SYSTEM

PROACTIVE – PROFESSIONAL – POSITIVE – PERSISTENT

CHAPTER SIX
GROWTH
NETWORKING & WRITER ORGANIZATIONS

Why is this important to your business? Growth requires one to continually work on learning and improving. This means honing your skills. It means keeping up with industry changes. This is best done by learning from and networking with your peers.

Writers are generally (not me) introverts and have chosen a solitary business. We sit at our computers day in and out writing fantasies that come to us—in my case, in our dreams—or when we should be sleeping.

We need to find our tribes, our people, those of like mind who understand what we're going through. We need to connect with peers we can relate to. We can learn from each other and find relief in the fact others are going through and understand our complex worlds. In my case, I'm an extrovert, so this is essential for me.

I've found writers to be the most giving and helpful people I've had the opportunity to work with. Authors are extremely busy, trying to balance personal lives, our own health and well-being, families, writing careers, business requirements, and sometimes another career. It's taxing, sometimes frustrating.

In our writing lives, we're juggling networking time, volunteer time with writing groups, marketing, social media, with finding time to write. It takes perseverance and a strong will to do all of this.

Joining the right professional group can provide not only that ability to spend time with like-minded people—your clan and learn from each other. It can lead to finding the right critique group and beta readers. You can gain access to affordable classes that can mean the difference between becoming a bland so-so writer and becoming a professional, well-rounded, author turning out books that keep readers flipping pages.

I belong to several organizations where I find the lifeblood of the industry thrives. Among the many are a few of the ones I participate in.

- Sisters In Crime
- The Derby Rotten Scoundrels, Ohio Valley Chapter SiC
- Mystery Writers of America
- Romance Writers of America
- Kiss of Death, Chapter RWA
- Mystery Writers of America
- Contemporary Romance Writers

Some organizations provide incredible learning opportunities for extremely low costs or for free. Others have great critique groups or forums to learn from. Some provide a social outlet for authors who need support.

Most groups have yearly national conventions with expert speakers and workshops on many subjects pertaining to writing. They provide opportunities to network and meet people who can help with your business growth.

Many offer world-renowned opportunities to enter contests judged by agents and publishers, which could help you make contacts to get your works published. They provide opportunities to win accolades or receive quotable reviews and valuable professional advice. These things can help when you market your books.

You choose how much or how little to engage in your groups, but all professional organizations offer major benefits. Their websites should provide details about them. Take advantage of these great resources.

I highly recommend you shop around for at least one group you can join and benefit from. I'm providing a handout with a list of some professional organizations you might want to check out. (See the Handout Page.)

EDUCATION

The industry and expectations of style and manuscript formatting have changed dramatically over the years. In this ever-changing world of publishing, it is essential to continually stay informed. Without a knowledge of industry expectations, you have little chance of being published.

No matter what your college degree is, it is important to realize none of us knows everything. We can learn something from others and continual study

I find it helpful to take as many classes each year as I can work into my busy schedule and seek out classes, videos, and podcasts offered by authors and writing organizations that might fill gaps of my skills and knowledge base. These groups offer a vast variety of informative subjects. I take at least 3-4 each year and have never attended a class where I didn't learn at least one actionable thing.

Reading the work of others is an education. Read the genre you write about as well as others of interest to you, especially the latest works of those authors you admire

Continual education to hone craft and stay in tune with the publishing industry has proved vital to my writing career, as I assure you, it will yours. You've taken that first step by being here today.

HOMEWORK:

1. Make a list of things you would like to learn. Check into classes through your or other writing organizations to see what they cost and when they are available.
2. Check with your writing organization to see if they sponsor a yearly convention. Put it on your calendar and plan to attend if you can.

REMEMBER THE 4 P SYSTEM

PROACTIVE – PROFESSIONAL – POSITIVE - PERSISTENT

CHAPTER SEVEN
KEEPING IT STRAIGHT
MANUSCRIPTS AND FILES (See Handout Page)

If you publish with a small or large-press publishing house, you will be assigned an editor. It may or may not be the person who brought you into the contract with the publisher.

Most publishing houses send your book through two-to-three rounds of editing looking for holes in the story, things that are missed or in the wrong place, or confusing content. He or she is looking for ways to strengthen the book, so it thrills your audience.

It's important to save a copy of every version—original, each edit you do, each edit suggestion version from your editor and publisher and your final version, in case you need to refer to something that was removed or changed. You can do this by establishing a folder for editing and using the Save and Save As option naming each version something that makes sense and the date.

For example:

HOTM V1 LR 010123 which are the initials of my book Heart of the Matter, the version number, my initials because I am the approver of this edit, and the date approved. I might call the version by my editor HOTM V2 LJP 010223.

Editing is generally done in Word using the Tracking section of Review. It helps keep track of who suggests what, who accepts or rejects changes in each round, and what you approve of or reject.

Why bother? It could be important for you to maintain records of each version of the story as it is written, edited, and formatted. Ensure the changes made are ones you approved and nothing else. It's easy for a formatter to omit a chapter, word, or scene, especially at the end of a chapter. Inspect the work. Make sure this doesn't happen.

When you approve the final version before it goes to press, use the last edited version to compare. Be sure nothing has been inadvertently changed or left out. This is your last chance.

Also, you might later want to use a piece of work in ads that you removed from the manuscript. It could be useful in interviews or marketing. Just because it's not best used in the final publication doesn't mean it can't be intriguing to a reader and encourage them to purchase your book.

This is how I keep track of all that. I created a folder for the story. Inside that, I create a folder for the cover, one for the manuscript, another for marketing tools, etc.

Under Manuscript I have the final versions of each format, the proofs I download as the files are loaded to distributors, and the edited and formatted versions. Here's an example of how I manage files. The example is also in handout form.

EXAMPLE OF FILE SYSTEM FOR BOOK
INFORMATION WRITING
BOOKS
The Bloodline Series
Parsley, Sage, Rose, Mary & Wine

- Audio
- Blurbs - Synopsis
- Ad Publicity Marketing
- Ads
- Art
- Book Trailer
- Videos and Gifs
- Contests
- Press Kit
- Videos
- Cover
- Manuscript
- Editing Versions
- Formatted Versions
- Published Versions
- eBooks (epub mobi)
- Proofs
- Print
- Proofs
- Audiobooks
- Auditions
- Contracts
- Clips
- Submissions (Folder for each agency/publisher)
- Translations
- Spanish
- French
- German
- Italian
- Research

Blood & Studs (Includes similar files to PSRM&W.)
Hot Blooded (Includes similar files to PSRM&W.
Blood of Champions (Includes similar files to PSRM&W.)

Reggie Chronicles
Hart's Girls
Heart of the Matter
Magnolia Blossoms
Stand Alone Books
2nd Chance Ranch
Operation Second Chance
Gold Lust Conspiracy
Flip or Flop, Murder House
Fresh Starts, Dirty Money
Children
Freckle Face & Blondie
The Thinking Tree
NO FEAR
Fear Learning & Activity Book
Non-Fiction
(etc. with remaining books and series.)

<u>HOMEWORK (Should you decide to accept the challenge):</u>

1. Organize and Color Code your hard copy files.
2. Organize your virtual file system. Create online folders and subfolders by book and subject. Move your online files into them.

REMEMBER THE 4 P SYSTEM

PROACTIVE – PROFESSIONAL –
POSITIVE - PERSISTENT

CHAPTER EIGHT

CHARACTERS PROFILES (See Handout Page for template.)

You might wonder why such in-depth detail is important. There are so many reasons, I'm afraid I might not be able to capture them all but let me try.

First, learning who the people you are writing about are in great depth enables you to understand how they tick. What makes them act and react in a certain manner? What they have faced causes them to feel the way they do. Why do they fear or dread something? What hurts them emotionally and physically? Understanding the person enables you to capture their true essence in your story and engage the reader so they love and hate—feel both emotions about this person. This creates an unforgettable character.

It draws the reader into the story and holds their attention. This helps you be a better writer and to avoid nasty letters from fans who catch your mistakes. Don't think they won't. Readers are smart. They will know if your hero has a lisp in the first story and doesn't in the others. They'll catch you if you give him a different high school or color of eyes at some point, or if he no longer has an accent or way of speaking. I don't want to forget that Justin Henderson has a prosthesis on his left leg and suddenly his limp goes the other direction. My fans would definitely catch that.

Once the story is written, this character diary helps in many other ways. You might decide to follow the first with a series of books.

You might think you will remember your hero's scar was on his left cheek or that he picks his cuticles. After a period of time and working on other books, it's difficult to recall all the specifics.

Here are a few pictures of some of my book boyfriends. Meet Eli, Wyatt, Justin Henderson, Cal, Moggie, Clay, Leo, and Sam. These are only a few, so you can see how difficult it might become to recall the color of their eyes, how they speak, how they react, what their hot points are, what motivations they might have, what pains each of them, drives them, etc.

This is why I recommend creating a book diary for each book and/or series with a page for each character. You will find yourself constantly referring to your diary. Use it when you write blurbs, back copy, advertising, etc.

You will use it repeatedly. My first book diary is a ragged, worn, spiral notebook with curly pages from wear and tear. I no longer hand write in a notebook. Now I capture information on a Word document. I print the pages when the book is finished and put them into a notebook. That way all that data is available at my fingertips. I find having it in print is extremely helpful and saves me tons of time.

Visuals of some more of my book boyfriends. You can see how difficult it becomes to keep track of all the tiny details. This isn't even the complete list, and it is only the male characters. There's an extensive group of female characters to keep track of as well.

Meet Dex, Eli, Chance, Justin Martin, Shea, and Logan.
Homework:

1. Use the handout to create a character profile each for the hero and heroine of your work in progress.
2. Find a free stock image of someone who resembles your imaginary hero and heroine. Be sure to check the licensing requirements to make certain you don't infringe on the photographer's or model's legal rights to the image and how you are allowed to and not allowed to use it.
3. Purchase any model shots you want to use in artwork. Beware of using images of a famous person in your ads. Models and celebrities have strict legal rights to images of themselves and control of how they are used. It could prove to be a costly error on your part.
4. Let me know if you think this is helpful. Enjoy the process.

REMEMBER THE 4 P SYSTEM

PROACTIVE – PROFESSIONAL –
POSITIVE - PERSISTENT

CHAPTER NINE
PUBLISHING ROUTES AND SUBMISSIONS
ROUTE

You may choose to:

- Publish traditionally.
  - This can be done with a small-press publisher.
  - Or large-press publisher.
- Hire an agent.
  - Large-press publishers require submissions through agents.
  - Many small-press publishers do not generally require working with an agent. Some do.
- Hire an agent for certain things only.
  - Shopping your book for the film industry.
  - Selling your book to overseas publication
- Work directly with small press publishers.
- Indi-publish your work.
- Hybrid-publish. Any combination of the above.

YOUR ROLE
TRADITIONAL PUBLISHING

The publisher will provide editorial services. You will be expected to work with their editor to get to the final publishable format. The publisher will manage formatting, printing, and distribution without your help. They will choose the cover with or without input from you, depending on their flexibility and processes. They might possibly provide PR/Marketing resources that you will work with. Every company has their own expectations of how much feedback the author may contribute, and when and how it will be considered. No matter how you publish, you will be expected to establish an author platform and may receive help with that or at least guidance.

Marketing

Regardless of which route you choose; you will be heavily involved in the process of getting the word out to the public and industry that your book is available. If you're traditionally published, the company will guide this process. They will alert the industry of booksellers, distributors, and libraries of your publication and encourage them to stock your book.

The publisher will determine the manner and amount of funds to a decided limit what is spent to market your book.

They may provide you with options you can optimize to supplement their marketing plan.

If the publisher's plan includes PR and/or a book tour of sorts (today usually virtual), you will be expected to be available for book signings, readings, appearances, interviews, blogs, etc.

A small press publisher will have less money to spend on marketing your book, so they will expect you to take a more active role. They may do some marketing and/or PR, and they may provide a list of free or low-cost advertising options you can fund yourself. Clarify with your publisher up front in the contract what they will and won't do for you, and what is expected of you.

If you Indi-publish, this will be your responsibility, whether you do it yourself or hire a publicist or agency to do it for you. You will want to determine your budget and spend your money wisely to obtain the maximum bang for your buck.

There are many options available. You can do ads in Book-Bub, Goodreads, Facebook, Twitter, Amazon, Google, etc. Most social media venues and distribution outlets provide options for some types of paid advertising. My advice is, go for low-hanging fruit first. Take advantage of low-cost or free options. Start small. If you decide to run ads, test advertising before expanding to higher spending levels.

Of course, this depends on your budget and goal. It will require a large outlay to accomplish your goal if your intention is to become a Times Best Seller. So, before you launch, determine what your publisher is already doing, what you are willing to spend, and what your goal is.

THE "BIG FIVE"

If you're an excellent writer, have perfect timing, and hire a go-getter agent, you could get lucky enough to publish traditionally with one of the awesome "BIG FIVE" Publishers.

As of this publishing date, they are:

- Penguin/Random House
- Hachette Book Group
- Harper Book Group
- Simon and Schuster
- Macmillan

Contracts

Regardless of whether you sign with a Top Five Publisher or a small press publisher, be sure to consult an entertainment attorney and read the contract before signing anything. Understand exactly what rights you are signing over to the publishing company (eBook, print, audio, international, film rights, gaming, etc.).

Never sign a contract without completely understanding what you are selling. Contract language can be complex. It's meant to cover everything. If you don't understand something, you're not alone. Be sure to get clarification from your legal counsel to understand exactly what complicated legalese means.

Be sure you know how long the company will own the rights to the book. How long will it take them to get it to the market? How long will they keep it in publication? What are your royalties?

What happens to the rights should the company fold? Don't think it won't. Publishers go out of business all the time. They might be bought by another company. Be clear on how to retrieve your book rights should any of these things happen.

If you aren't lucky enough to go the route of a large-press publisher, don't despair. There are many other lucrative options to becoming a published author.

There are literally thousands of reputable small-press publishers. You can't do a search online or on social media without discovering a long list of small press publishers. Some of them require submissions by agents. Others are open to direct submissions from authors.

Allotment of Funds

Whether large or small, they have a budget and limited resources. They spread those people-assets and financial resources across the number of books they determine they can publish efficiently each year. This depends on their goals, strategies, and tactics. This bulk of capital is then split by the genres they wish to publish in.

Within each genre category, the bulk of resources naturally goes to proven authors with records of excellent sales. The publisher will likely also back authors with steady profitability, steady sales—ones they're grooming to become top sellers. These are first- and second-string authors. First-string authors will have more funds put toward their books. Second-string authors will have somewhat less funds spent to publish their works.

If a company's goal includes publishing new authors, the portion of budget and resources they allot to debut authors will be spread among the number they've chosen to work with. This group will have the most limited funds to work with.

For instance, there's a portion of resources and funds allotted to proven, successful authors. These are writers they've worked with previously, or who have a record elsewhere as a top seller. They may allot more money to this piece of the pie than to others, because they anticipate that money spent to provide the bulk of their profits

They may allot a slightly smaller amount of cash and people to work on up-and-coming authors, because data shows these people have profit growth potential, based on previous publishing. The company needs to grow these authors to eventually be moved into the Proven piece of the pie. They anticipate immediate profit from this group but maybe not as much as they will reap from the Proven category.

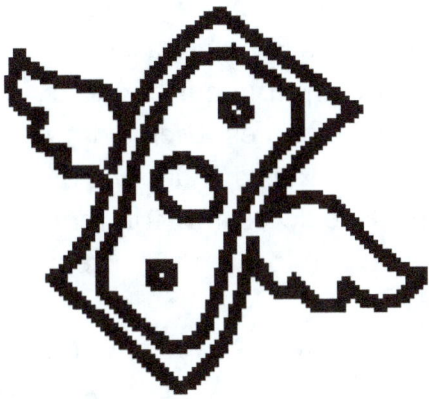

Finally, remaining resources and currency may be allotted to debut authors. This is a horse race. These writers have potential but no track record. It's like betting on a longshot at the racetrack. They believe they'll be winners and are willing to back them, but they're not sure what will happen.

You've heard the phrase, 'don't invest all your eggs in one basket.' In finance, this is what is meant by diversification. For maximum growth potential money should be spread across varied types of investments to reach maximum growth and protect investment from loss. Publishing companies use that same type of strategy to invest in publishing books. They are in the business of profits, no matter how beautiful your manuscript is written.

See example chart below.

Whether you're talking about a publisher or agent, the previous information applies in most cases.

Where do you find a publisher or agent?

There are many resources these days. Among those, I suggest you check out Reedsy, Query Tracker, Agent Query, Facebook, Twitter, Google search for agents/publishers. Ask your librarian to help you locate the current year's listing book published.

Remember this, however. Never pay a person or organization to read your submission. A legitimate agent or publisher will not ask for payment.

Yes. Vanity Publishers are out there, and some people choose to work with them. Personally, I'm not a fan. I've met very few authors who are. There are way too many legitimate publishers and agents who will read your work, looking for a gem they can make a profit from selling. It would benefit you to seek out one of these.

SUBMISSIONS

Before submitting your manuscript, it's important to study the company and/or agent to be sure they're legitimate and successful, and that they are looking for what you provide. Otherwise, you are wasting your time reaching out to them. Read all the details on their company website. Ask other authors about them. Have they had good or bad experiences with them, etc. What books like yours have they published? What is on their wish list. What are the submission guidelines.

If you fail to meet the submission guidelines in any way, whether formatted or submitted incorrectly, they will toss your manuscript into the trash file. These people are extremely busy with stacks of manuscripts to read received daily. Yours is like a needle in a haystack. If you can't be bothered to adhere to guidelines by the letter, they will assume your work is not up to par either. They will choose not to work with you.

SUBMISSION TRACKING (See Handout Page for template.)

If you're submitting your work to agents or publishers, waiting for word can be frustrating. These people are extremely busy. They have stacks of submissions to review every day. They have many published authors to manage, as well as reading submissions to discover new manuscripts or authors; and they have lives. Be patient. Don't bombard them asking if they've gotten to your manuscript yet. This is not a case where the squeaky wheel gets the attention—at least, not the kind of attention you want.

Your chances of success are better if you're organized and do the necessary research to learn what the specific agent, agency, or publisher wants. Study the company and/or agent, associate, or publisher. The more you know, the better your submission will be. This will help you meet their expectations, as you submit. If you don't, your submission will be tossed immediately into the trash file.

The wait and anticipation can become easier if you know what to expect. Keeping track of where, when, and to whom you send submissions can minimize frustration.

Most of these professionals' sites post on their sites how long it should take for them to get back to you. They'll usually advise whether they will let you know if your work is or is not being requested and how you can check on the status of your submission.

If the website says they respond in 10 days, 3 months, or 6 months, knowing that will help reduce your anxiety. Do not bother them before that time has elapsed. When and if you follow up, be sure to do it in a professional manner.

If they advise that they do not respond unless they want more or to work with you, feel free to check back with them; but it's safe to assume they have decided to pass on your work for some reason. Move on.

Others respond to every submission. Sometimes it's a form letter. Other times it's a note explaining why they're passing. It isn't always your work, but sometimes what they are able to do, what they are already working on, or just doesn't fit their goals for the specific year. Don't be disheartened. Just move on to the next one on your list.

If they want more, they will always reach out to request it via email. DO NOT expect a phone call unless you are being offered a contract. Even that is sometimes offered via email, usually with a follow up call to discuss any questions you or they have.

Tracking will ensure you know what is happening with your manuscript. It will ensure you don't send multiple submissions of the same work to a company. This is a definite No No.

Tracking will also help you budget your time and plan the date to send out more submissions if you do not receive an offer, or to publish the work on your own as an indie-author.

I've provided a template for the spreadsheet I use to track submissions. I hope it's helpful to you.

REMEMBER THE 4 P SYSTEM

PROACTIVE – PROFESSIONAL – POSITIVE - PERSISTENT

CHAPTER TEN
INDIE-PUBLISHING OVERVIEW

There are many outlets for you to publish your books yourself, should you decide to become an independent author. This can be done in all formats (eBook, paperback, hardback, large-print, and audiobook). Where you choose to publish is your choice. Not all Indi-publishers provide all formats. For instance, check out the following outlets.

If you're Indie-published, you manage every single aspect of the publishing process. This doesn't mean you must take each step yourself. It means you choose how to manage each step. You can do it alone, or you can hire people to do certain steps you don't choose to execute alone.

Self-publishing is a multi-step, complex route with a learning curve. Basic steps are:

- book cover designing.
- editing
- formatting
- publishing/distribution/printing

- marketing
- publicity/public relations
- launches and book tour scheduling/management.

You can do every chore on your own once you obtain the right skills. Or you can hire professionals to do those things you don't know how to do, don't have time to do, or don't want to do

Professionals

Experts in each field are readily available to help bring your manuscript into a publishable format. Or you can do the work yourself. The question is

- What can you afford to pay for?
- What do you like doing.
- What do you hate working on?
- How much time do you have available?
- What is your time worth?
- What route is the most effective and efficient?

Jobs

These are the basic job descriptions for steps in the publishing process. We'll go over each of them individually.

- Editor (There are several types.)
- Formatter
- Book Cover Designer
- Publicist, Marketing, Public Relations
- Publishing/Distribution Management

We are going to cover each of these, but not in sequence order.

DISTRIBTUION

IngramSpark, recently joined hands with Spotify and allows you to publish eBooks, print, and hardcopy through them. They do not provide an audiobook option at this time. They manage printing, distribution and royalties paid through them. IngramSpark distributes books to a wide range of publishers, including Apple, B&N, Kindle, etc. If you pay a fee to have your book in their catalog, your book will be available for purchase by booksellers and libraries. Here's the link to check out where all they distribute.

https://www.ingramspark.com/blog/book-distribution-with-ingramspark

Previously you could pay an up-front fee and publish eBooks, print and hardbacks with IngramSpark. They have since moved to a percentage-based fee for publishing through them, similar to other distributors.

IngramSpark is my preferred way of publishing eBooks and Print, especially print and hard copies. You can also publish hardback books through them. The reason I prefer this distribution route is their vast network of distribution and that they make their publications available to libraries.

Their printer is Lightning Source. Royalties paid through them comes from Lighting Source.

If you choose to publish separately to each distributor (like Kindle, Apple, B&N, KOBO/Walmart, etc.), you are able to do that. However, like IngramSpark, they charge a percentage of the royalties for sales. Each company offers deals for special marketing options if you go exclusively with them, but they do not require exclusivity. This may work for you, or you may choose to 'go wide.' This means uploading separately to each distributor without exclusivity. This takes time, but it may be the most profitable.

Each case is unique. Everyone has a different opinion on this. I won't tell you how you should distribute your book. My aim is to give you an idea of what is available to you. You can publish in one place or 'go wide.' Publish to as many distribution outlets as you wish. There are many resources to publish your own work.

How and where you distribute depends on you and your goals.

Regardless of the route, someone must upload a print-ready manuscript and cover to whatever system(s) you choose to use for distribution to readers.

IngramSpark makes your book available to most other distributors through their system, and you receive the portion of royalties that retailer provides, paid through Lightning Source. To get full distribution when publishing through IngramSpark you must sign an agreement for them to share the books with Amazon and one so they can share them with Barnes & Noble. IngramSpark offers an opportunity upon publishing to put your book in their catalogue, which makes it available to libraries and other distributors. Always check their terms and conditions, because they may have added new agreement forms that must be signed. These things are always subject to change in the crazy, ever-evolving publishing world.

There's no fee for publishing through Amazon KDP, KOBO, Barnes & Noble, Apple, Smashwords, Google Play for eBooks or print. As with most distributors, royalties are a portion of the whole; and the rest goes to the distributor. Agreements are online on their websites, along with guidelines and expectations. Distribution through these outlets is a simple process. There are other similar publishers outside of these. I personally have no experience with them.

You can upload your manuscript individually to each distributor (E.g., Kindle/Amazon, KOBO/Rakuten, B&N, Apple, Google Play, etc.), if you choose to go wide and don't sign up for exclusive distribution by any of them and don't use IngramSpark to publish. This is time consuming, but it might work for you. I've done it before discovering IngramSpark. I prefer IngramSpark because I do not have to spend time up-loading to each site separately.

If you want to go exclusive with your eBook, you can up-load to Kindle Amazon and go Kindle Unlimited. KU provides options to put your book on sale, to advertise through them for free every 3 months, or to host a temporary 'giveaway' option to readers. You also have the option to receive bonuses should you earn any. This is an exclusive distribution agreement, so be sure to read the details of the contract before committing. It is possible to opt in for a specific period of time and then step out of the program, however.

When I first started, I had no idea how to format manu-scripts for Kindle mobi eBooks, eBooks for elsewhere in epub, or for print versions. I hired Marie Force's Formatting Fairies to format and to upload my formatted work to Apple. At that time, Apple required uploads from a MAC computer. That is no longer an issue. I now do my own Apple uploading. Also, mobi is no longer required for Kindle publishing. They have gone the way of other distributors and now use epub format-ted versions.

There are other similar resources for self-publishing. You might want to Google Indi-publishing or self-publishing. Be sure to read details by distributors you are considering using them, to ensure they provide what you want from their service and at a cost you are happy with.

As I previously mentioned, I do not recommend working with a vanity publisher. This merits restating. A vanity pub-lisher might charge a fee to read your book, to edit it, and to publish it. They might require you to purchase a set number of books from them. This can become pricey. I haven't met an author yet who was happy going the vanity publishing route. Beware, there are many out there and once you're publishing, they will seek you out. If you receive an offer that sounds the least bit suspicious, ask your peers about the company.

eBooks are widely distributed by Kindle , Apple Books, Barnes & Noble, Scribd, KOBO/Walmart, IngramSpark, Smashboards, BookBaby, KITABOO, and Reedsy, just to name a few of the top distribution resources.

Most distributors these days print books on demand. This allows the industry to be more cost efficient. By not stocking a supply of printed books in a warehouse, as was done by distributors in the past, there is savings on everything from paper to ink, manpower, storage space, shipping, and postage. With print on demand, there is no waste. This cuts down on costs. In the electronic age where data is quickly accessible, orders are confirmed at the longest overnight. Printing generally takes only a few days. It's extremely cost-effective and gives the independent author the ability to provide print and even hardback books.

Hardback has been available from IngramSpark and Barnes & Noble for quite some time. Recently Kindle, BookBaby, and some others have gotten into the hardback market, also offering print-on-demand services.

Most distributors of paperback and hardback books offer the author at-cost publishing for a certain number of copies. This allows you as the author to purchase them without the markup for your own use. You can distribute these copies to reviewers, offer them to readers, or sell them at retail cost (or whatever cost you choose) at personal events. You will be charged shipping in addition to printing, but it's a good deal

HOMEWORK

1. Make a list of the formats you want to publish in (eBook, print, hardback, audiobook, large print, serial, game, movie, television series, other languages, etc.). Prioritize this list.

2. How do you want to publish (traditional, small press, agented/non-agency, Indi-publish, etc.)? Prioritize this list.

REMEMBER THE 4 P SYSTEM

PROACTIVE – PROFESSIONAL – POSITIVE - PERSISTENT

CHAPTER ELEVEN
PRODUCING A PUBLISHABLE MANUSCRIPT
EDITING:

Editing is something that no author likes to do. Believe me. I'm right there with you. Editing, however, is essential in order to make your book publishable and to create the work in a format readers will love.

I'm not here to teach editing, but I will give you a few pointers. Never self-edit your own book. That doesn't mean you should send your first draft to an editor. Don't waste their time and your or your publisher's money.

Let the book sit for a week or so. Go back and read it aloud. Reading out loud lets you hear errors you might otherwise miss.

Fill in any holes in the story. Make sure the tale flows in the right timeline so everything makes sense. Fix typos, grammar. Add in missing or incorrect words. Run the document through Word's review process and fix whatever the system finds.

Editing errors, I've made that drive me crazy now.

- Repeated information. Readers are smart. They only need to hear it once to get it. You may have several lovely, creative ways to say something, but a reader will get bored and believe you think they're too stupid to 'get it' the first time. Pick the best way and say it once.
- Repeated words. In a paragraph, sentence, or page, do not repeat words—unless there's no way around it. Constantly repeating text interrupts flow. Get a Thesaurus and use it.

- Edit-Out words add nothing to the story. By edit-out, I mean words that add nothing except word-count. Words that weaken the prose should be replaced by something stronger. Useless, over-used, non-meaningful terms or phrases should be edited out. Make your words count. For instance: just, that, then, that, the, also, almost, almost, about, up, down.
  - Example. *He sat down in a chair.* How else could he sit? Only down. Right?
  - Most of the time such words are not needed. Eliminate them. If you need a list of edit out words, I've collected and summarized editing tips. The list can be found on my website at https://www.lynda-reesauthor.com
- Constantly repeating a character's name. This is especially unnecessary in dialogue. People don't continually use someone's name when talking with them.
- Stay in deep POV. This subject needs a full class to cover it. What I will tell you is that staying in POV keeps the reader enthralled in the story from the character's viewpoint.
  - So, don't say things the person doesn't know, hear, or see.
  - Don't use words like knew, know, hear, heard, see, saw, felt, feel, etc.
  - These words put distance between the reader and character.
  - Instead, stay in the character's head and write what they know, hear, see, or feel.

Once you've edited the death out of the book and made it perfect,' it's time to let someone else destroy your beautiful baby. Yep, that's how you'll feel when you get tough feedback, but it's how you can make the story the best it can be.

Share the work with a critique group. You will get incredible, actionable advice from your critique group of writers. Take advantage of their expertise, skills, and learnings. You don't have to take every bit of advice, but overall, you should find it valuable. This is especially true if more than one person points out a specific deficit in the story.

After you've included the group's feedback, send the revision to a couple of beta readers. These people should be super fans of yours. They want the best from you and will enjoy helping you craft their favorite stories. Include revisions. You're ready for the next step.

Send your manuscript to a professional editor. If you're planning to publish through a publisher or use an agent, it's time to submit.

This professional editor could be recommended by other authors, a pro you've met at a conference, or someone recommended on your writing organization's website database.

If you can't afford to pay a seasoned editor, an English, Literature, or Composition teacher or professor might work.

Check your local colleges or high schools.

Your author organization should have a list on their website of approved editors. Ask your author friends for recommendations. Some authors have told me they've hired English college majors to edit their works.

You can also find editors for hire on https://FIVERR.com. Find a resource you can work with and afford.

There are different types of editors. They are:

Development Editors - These editors help a writer develop the overall structure of the book, content, organization, tone, author's voice, and character development.

Copy Editors - These editors are concerned with finding errors in grammar and punctuation and awkward phrasing.

Line Editors - A line editor looks for grammar, spelling, and punctuation mistakes, so they are similar to a copy editor.

Substance Editors – These folks go past copy editing and look for clarity and style. They can help with rephrasing anything from sentences to entire chapters.

Proofreaders – These people look at the final version of a work for formatting issues and grammatical errors. Think of this as the last step in editing.

Some publishers have different titles such as managing editor, acquisitions editor, production editor or editor in chief. They are usually management positions versus actual editors.

FORMATTING:

You cannot simply upload your Word document manuscript to distributors' websites to publish it. Once your work is edited, you must be put into a format that meets the retailer's specifications for publishing eBooks, print, and hard copy versions. Each is different.

A print book requires a pdf formatted to specs and with fonts imbedded in the document.

An eBook requires an epub or possibly a mobi version formatted to specs, though mobi is becoming obsolete. Amazon Kindle recently updated their specs to require an epub format, slightly different from others.

Barnes &Noble and many other sites require the book be in epub format.

Apple iBooks allows epub uploading.

A retailer may require different specs from other retailers. Be sure to comply with their individual requirements. Otherwise, your upload will be rejected. Some retailers provide a template you can simply copy/paste your work into. This simplifies the process somewhat.

When I first started as an Indi-Author, I hired Marie Force's Formatting Fairies to do this step. Here's their link: Fairies Home Page - Marie Force

There are many resources to get this work done. I found Marie Forces' people to be quick, efficient, and pleasant to work with.

The https://FIVERR.com website also has formatters for hire. I have hired illustrators from this site but never formatters.

It was well worth the money to have my manuscripts formatted by a professional unless you are skilled in this area. Formatting is time-consuming and complex, and at that time I had no idea how to do it or desire to learn. I have since acquired skills to format my work myself.

If you prefer to learn to format your manuscript yourself, instructions are available to download from the KDP website. I've found it simple to format print versions of manuscripts using these instructions.

KDP also has templates available for eBook depending on the size you want to create. You can download the template size you choose for your book and drop text into it, and then upload the formatted book to KDP for publishing and they have tools to help format eBooks.

IngramSpark and B&N each have downloadable instructions for formatting their specs. Once you start uploading your book, they offer the opportunity to download the format template so you can drop the book data into it.

I prefer Scrivener for formatting eBooks in both epub and mobi forms and use Kindle's instructions for print format. I find Scrivener's print formatting is awkward. Others love it. It is a versatile tool. Do whatever you prefer.

Once the work is properly formatted, it must be uploaded to a distributor or distributors. Where you upload depends on your budget and goal.

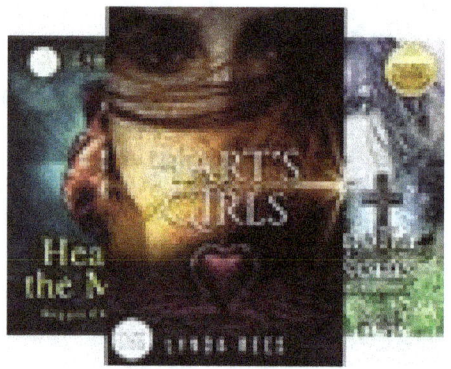

COVERS

A cover can make or break your book's success. A success-ful cover needs three things.

1. Stopping Power: You've got no more than three seconds to stop a shopping reader.
2. Genre clarity: Unless you want to disappoint your reader, the book cover should say visually what genre the book is.
3. Branding. Branding is the look and feel of the book. It is a way to make it recognizable as your book.

How do you achieve the look and feel, and how do you visualize genre, while creating branding?

Choose a font that fits what you write. Be sure it's easy to read. Many people make the mistake of choosing a fancy font that is literally illegible from a distance or without a magnifying glass.

Title and Author Name size and placement should be in the same locations. If not for all your books, placement should be the same at least for a series.

Your goal is to create an impression so readers can tell at a glance the book is one of yours and the type of book you write.

You will need a cover version for each format you publish in, as each requires different specs.

- eBook cover
- Print cover - front, back and spine.
- Hardback cover—front, back and spine
- Audiobook

These need to be specific pixel sized in high resolution. You will probably need versions for advertising in low res. Low-res images in sizes appropriate for online usage can be used for your website, emails, and social media. Once you have the image in high resolution, you can change the size of it yourself to create low-res copies for these purposes.

Ad visuals might include backgrounds, other related visuals or include advertising copy. You might want to have your art designer create them for you, or you could create them in PowerPoint and then convert them to jpg or png format using Paint. You can also create great ad versions in Canva if you have access to it.

Most advertising images will be in low res. However, if you have a large banner printed, you might need to provide the printer with a hi-res version of the image.

Your art designer can provide them in jpg, pdf and png format, depending on how you intend to use them. Clarify what they will provide for the price quoted.

COST- Covers are usually provided by your publisher. Sometimes they ask for or will include your input. Sometimes they don't. It's their preference. They are looking for a cover that will sell the book, one that clarifies the overall tone and character of the story and sets it apart in the genre or category it is placed in. Control of ownership and the process for development of the cover should be clarified in the contract, so you know beforehand what to expect. Regardless of your input, they will make the final decision.

If you're Indi-published, you will need to provide your covers. A front cover jpg is required to publish an eBook. The same front cover, with a back cover and spine, are required to publish a print book. The number of pages and size of the printed book must be determined before development of the spine for the print book.

If you choose to print in hard copy, there will need to be a 3rd version for this format developed, as printer specs for hard copies are different for hard copies.

Covers can be expensive, especially if you have them specifically designed from scratch to your specifications. I do not recommend you design your own covers unless you are a professional artist. Hire a pro to design this extremely important tool

Covers can be relatively inexpensive if you make use of the many pre-designed covers available. The websites that house pre-made covers usually show only the eBook cover. If you choose one and need a hardback cover and/or advertising visuals in other formats, the artist should be available to create these additional forms at desirable cost.

As an indie-published author, you have three options.

1. Buy a stock art piece to use in software like the cover creator on KDP or Canva to design the cover. I don't recommend this, personally. I feel mor comfortable with

a professionally designed cover, and that has served me well.

2. Work with an artist to design from scratch, something specifically for you and your brand and/or series. This is the most expensive route but may in the long run be the best for you. General cost can range from a couple hundred dollars upward of a thousand, depending on what you want them to do. If a photo shoot is required, it's going to be expensive. Results should be awesome, however.

3. Purchase a pre-made cover. There are thousands of them available. I've done this for many books and worked with artists to create others. This is my favorite source. A great number of artists specialize in every genre you can think of and make their works available. They are quick to respond and make requested changes. This has proved extremely efficient, relatively low cost, and the artists are very professional.

Some pre-made book cover sources:

https://thebookcoverdesigner.com/product-category/pre-made-book-covers/

https://bookcoverzone.com/

https://www.premadeebook

There are many others. These are only a few I've checked. Artists who work with these companies also usually have their own websites where they may feature other covers and premium services. If you don't find what you need at one, you will likely find it at another.

Costs can range from $20 to $200 and up, depending on what elements you want to purchase from them (e.g., advertising shots, bundles, series packages, etc.).

Either way, when working with an artist, respect their time. Be clear up front what you want them to do. If you don't it can become costly and take additional rounds at your expense to fix problems you have created by providing them with unclear instructions in the beginning.

If you're working with a design artist to create a cover from scratch, I suggest using a design brief. This is a tool that allows you to provide guidance in a language the artist can find actionable. This will provide clarity and help prevent errors or misconceptions about what you are looking for them to do for you.

Design Brief (See Handout Page for template

I am providing a design brief template for you. Feel free to use it for your artwork projects.

Start with a paragraph giving an overview of your expectations. Cover the scope of what you want. Before you begin, close your eyes. Imagine exactly what you want the finished product to look like. What do you need to tell the artist so they can create that image. This is the complete scope of the project.

Remember, however, you have hired an expert—an artist. They will interpret what you have told them you want and return it to you in an artistic manner. Don't tell them how to do it. Tell them what you want, and they will interpret your needs in a creative way and create that visual image.

Your brief doesn't have to be long and wordy. A clear, focused summation of what you are thinking should be your goal when writing the creative brief. After all, it's called a *brief* for a reason.

The better the brief, the better the finished product will be, and the artist will be able to meet your request more efficiently. A clear, concise brief helps save time for both of you and saves you money.

- Do you want them to design a front cover only or a print version for a book with 300 pages in a 5" x 8" paperback printed on white or beige paper
- Do you need a hardback version?
- What is the size, color paper, and number of pages?
- Explain what the tone should be, your goals for the book, the audience and if there are specific visuals you want in it.
- Do you want something that looks romantic, sexy, sweet, scary, mysterious, or mystic?

- Who is the competition?
- What similar author writes books comparable to yours?
- Will you need advertising artwork that is large enough to produce a huge banner, or just something that can be used for small ads, banners, signs, business cards, book-marks, and online advertising?
- Is there a bio or review you want on the back?
- Are certain images (attached) to be used?
- Is there a specific font that should be used.
- Are there specific colors that should be used?
- What is the priority of communication (Title vs. Subtitle, vs. Author Name, vs. Imagery)? Provide these items.
- What is the back cover copy?
- How and when can they reach you with any questions?

HOMEWORK:

1. Do a search in my favorite book cover seller under the genre of your WIP. Scan the covers available in your genre. See if you can find one that might work for your book. Sometimes, even if you're not the one who will choose the final image, it helps during the writing process to get

an idea of what the cover presented to the public might look like.

2. Make a list of five pros and five cons to each form of publishing. Consider which route you might want to take once your book is finished. No worries. You have time to change your mind. It's never too late, until the contract is signed.

REMEMBER THE 4 P SYSTEM

PROACTIVE – PROFESSIONAL – POSITIVE - PERSISTENT

CHAPTER TWELVE
TRACKING
SYSTEM NUMBERS

How do readers, libraries, booksellers, and others in the industry find your book? Yes, you have a title, and they can search for that. They can also search for books by your name. Title and name may or may not be exclusive to you. For instance, there's another author by my name in Ireland. I've written books then seen others publish using my same title— exactly. It's frustrating.

Before naming your book, be sure to search everywhere for the title. If it's broadly used or used elsewhere, you may want to rethink it. Try to go not only for something that speaks to the book matter and genre but for as unique a name as possible.

The world of publishing works on numbers not titles or author names. It's the way it is. These numbers need tracking for your books. There are two basic types.

ISBNs and BISAC (See Handout Page.)

If you're going to market through a traditional means, the publisher will generally purchase the ISBN and categorize your book via BISAC codes (see handout). They may or may not share this information with you. If you're Indi-publishing, it will be up to you to do so.

International Standard Book Numbers

NUMBER	NAME	TYPE	DATE
978-0-6900663-3-3	Pr8DaWa	Paperback	2017
978-0-6900663-1-0	Cold Lash Conspiracy	Paperback	2017

ISBN or International Standard Book Numbers are one-of-a-kind numbers that identify each specific edition of a title or book format from a publisher. A different one would be used for a paperback version vs. a hardback version. A unique one can be used for an audiobook version, and another for the eBook version (if you choose an ISBN), and a different one for a large-print version. If a book is republished under a second edition, that would require a new ISBN number.

These unique identifiers enable buyers at retailers, libraries, and shoppers to find your book quickly. ISBNs can be purchased from https://Bowker.com .

Amazon Kindle may provide an ISBN when you publish through them. The same is true of other distributors like Barnes & Nobel, etc. However, a distributor-provided ISBN will only be unique to the version published with that retailer. You don't own it. If you publish through several retailers and they provide the ISBN numbers for your books, the same book version will have as many different ISBNs as retailers you publish with. This can make it complicated for a retail outlet book buyer, a librarian, and sometimes for a reader to find your book.

If you purchase the ISBN from Bowker that is used for your book, you own it and can use it with all retailers across the board. This simplifies the process. It also means you can include that number in the copywrite page of the front matter.

Every print book requires an ISBN number, whether you purchase one or let the distributor provide it. eBooks do not require ISBN numbers; however, you can assign one so it's easier for your book to be found by those searching via that number.

BISAC

A BISAC is a Book Industry Standards and Communication code. BISAC codes are nine-digit alphanumeric codes that tell book retailers, distributors, and librarians what categories and subcategories a book belongs in. It is standard across publishing worldwide.

Google BISAC to find a complete list of codes. I've provided an EXCEL spreadsheet as a handout listing of BISAC codes. Note, this list may be updated on a need-to basis by those who manage it. This one is merely a snapshot as of this date of printing. This BISAC is not a number you can own. It is a number you or your publisher assigns to the book, so the industry knows where in the market your book falls.

Your publisher will determine the correct BISAC code for your book. If you're Indi-published, you may need to determine that on your own, especially if you publish through Ingram-Spark or other such retailers. It's not necessary to determine the BISAC code when publishing directly through Kindle, B&N, or some other retailers such as those.

Below is an example of a few categories, genres, and sub-genres within the BISAC code system.

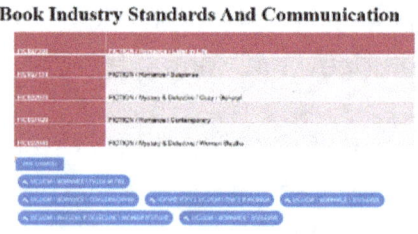

Book Industry Standards And Communication

For instance, for my books I might select these BISAC codes.

FIC027380	FICTION / Romance / Later in Life
FIC027110	FICTION / Romance / Suspense
FIC022070	FICTION / Mystery & Detective / Cozy / General
FIC027020	FICTION / Romance / Contemporary
FIC022040	FICTION / Mystery & Detective / Women Sleuths

I get it. They sound like ISBN numbers. You're right, and they are similar. The difference is that you or the publisher you work with own the ISBN unique identifier. You cannot own a BISAC code. It is simply a filing mechanism, so your book is put into the right section or category for others to find.

Below is an example of a few BISAC codes.

MYSTERY

FIC022000FICTION / Mystery & Detective / General

FICTION / Mystery & Detective / African American *see* African American / Mystery & Detective

FIC022100FICTION / Mystery & Detective / Amateur Sleuth

FIC022050FICTION / Mystery & Detective / Collections & Anthologies

FIC022070FICTION / Mystery & Detective / Cozy / General

FIC022110FICTION / Mystery & Detective / Cozy / Cats & Dogs

FIC022120FICTION / Mystery & Detective/Cozy /Crafts

FIC022130FICTION / Mystery & Detective / Cozy / Culinary

FIC022010FICTION / Mystery & Detective / Hard-Boiled

FIC022060FICTION / Mystery & Detective / Historical

FIC022080**FICTION** / Mystery & Detective / International Crime & Myster

FIC022020**FICTION** / Mystery & Detective / Police Procedural

FIC022090**FICTION** / Mystery & Detective / Private Investigators

FIC022030**FICTION** / Mystery & Detective / Traditional

FIC022040**FICTION** / Mystery & Detective / Women Sleuths

ROMANCE

FIC027000**FICTION** / Romance / General

FIC027260**FICTION** / Romance / Action & Adventure

FIC049060**FICTION** / Romance / African American

KEY WORDS

Wording is another way of helping readers locate your book easily. When shopping, most readers search via words. This could be anything from a short phrase like "smalltown romance" to a famous author's name, to a descriptor like "trafficking.

This is a complex topic I can't fully cover here. I will give you the basics to spur your thinking. I suggest you go to Amazon Kindle's site and under Help, search for "Key Words." They have a ton of valuable information to learn from.

To make shopping and locating your book easier for potential readers, you will want to learn to use key words that are frequently searched on. Amazon has some great tools you should check out. Go to their Help section and type Key Word

Search. If you think a key word is fitting, go into the Amazon online store under books and search for that word. See how many pop up.

You may be looking for words that have high traffic. In the case of a niche-type book, you might score higher on searches if you choose words that fit the niche clearly. It's a balancing act.

If you find that the key words you originally use to publish aren't doing their job, you can always go back in and change them to something more unique or findable.

ASIN

Kindle assigns a number called an ASIN or Amazon System Inventory Number, for each eBook published through them. Your eBook can be located via searching that number. ISBNs are not required to publish eBooks via Kindle/Amazon or some other online retailers.

ASINs are Kindle company inventory numbers only. They are not relevant outside of the Kindle/Amazon marketplace. Th ASIN is used only for eBooks on Amazon, whether they have an ISBN or not.

I'm not sure why, but Amazon does not apply an ASIN for print or hardback books. I believe it has to do with an outside printing source that prints on demand as books are ordered, so these books are not stocked in Amazon's online or physical warehouse.

PROMO CODES

If you publish audiobooks, you will want to secure free audiobook promotion codes. I've provided a spreadsheet that might help you track which ones you've given out and those still available. These are available through ACX as well as through Spotify. They allow your readers to download audio versions of your books for free.

These are not for sale. They are to help you promote your book and secure reviews. Send them to reviewers, to your beta reader group and other devoted readers. Share them as gifts or promo prizes to readers. Be sure to ask the receivers to review your book. You will get better results if you provide the review link along with the request.

HOMEWORK:

1. Pull the BIASC report up and determine what categories would be best to publish your work-in-progress in.
2. Search for Key Words that might fit your book using the Amazon tools.
3. Take a look at eBooks in your genre under Amazon and look for their ASIN numbers.
4. Go to the Bowkers site and check out the options available for purchasing ISBNs for your work.

REMEMBER THE 4 P SYSTEM

PROACTIVE – PROFESSIONAL –
POSITIVE - PERSISTENT

CHAPTER THIRTEEN
MARKETING

Most traditional publishers spend the greatest amount of time and money on well-known authors. They spend considerably less or little-to-nothing on an unknown author.

Unless you're in the first category, be prepared to receive a list of marketing resources from your publisher's publicist. Even if you're a big-time author, they will require you to participate in the marketing they do.

In most cases, you will need to do much of it on your own and with your own money. Make sure you are not overlapping or duplicating their efforts but putting out additional awareness.

COST vs. VALUE

Over time, as your brand grows to a position of recognition, you may find you may be able to spend less on marketing and advertising. It's not necessary to be a major player in the industry to have a strong brand and lucrative market presence.

Here's some data that might be of interest to you.

- In 2012-22 by category book publisher sales revenue in the U. S. (*Published 6/19/23 by Amy Watson of Statista*)
  - The adult category remained most lucrative in terms of revenue generating over 5.76 billion U.S. dollars in 2022, with children's books falling slightly between 2021 and 2022.
- 33% of book buyers are searching for new authors. This is according to The Romance Book Buyer study by NPD Book for Romance Writers of America. (*Methodology:*

Smpl 2M rom. Book readers 12/2017. Gender and age quota nat. rep. smpl. rom. bk. readers.

- Net revenue of the U.S. print book publishing industry was 28.1 billion USD.
- Audiobook sales revenue in the U.S. was 1.8 billion USD, showing continued growth.
- eBook sales in the U. S. were 198 million USD, showing continued growth.

I don't know about you, but I'd be happy with ½ a percentage of that money. For adult eBooks alone, just in the USA, that would be $955M. For audiobooks that would be $90M. For print that would be $1405MM. Total of all three is $2,495MM. I think I'd be really happy with just a half of a percentage of those sales at two-and-a-half-billion dollars a year. So, you see, you don't have to obtain a large portion of the market in order to be financially successful.

BRAND STRATEGY DRIVES GROWTH

In the publishing industry, as the data in the last section shows, it's not necessary to be concerned about authors having acquired market share and being well-established in the marketplace.

Though they may be well-positioned brand can still retain loyalty among its customer base, readers are always looking to read from new authors.

You can also achieve sales goals by diversifying your offerings by adding different forms of your books. For example, add a hardback cover book if you only have paperback. Add an eBook and/or audiobook. If you write non-fiction, add a workshop or online class. You can also create more compelling solutions with bundles.

Sometimes simply refreshing or reshaping your brand or relaunching with a new cover might help spur growth. Give your readership reasons to buy more.

When you launch a new book in-line with your overall brand, it helps customers see the change as a next step in their journey with you as an author.

Managing your brand's consistency requires effort but gets easier over time as readers become more familiar with how your brand manifests across different books, media, and touch-points. The investment is minimal compared to the returns it provides for your overall business value.

> **REMEMBER THE 4 P SYSTEM**
>
> **PROACTIVE – PROFESSIONAL – POSITIVE - PERSISTENT**

CHAPTER FOURTEEN
LAUNCHES / TOURS / PUBLIC RELATIONS

Lee Pennington, Archeologist, Author, Documentary Producer, Poet, and Lynda Rees, Author. My dear friend, Lee and I enjoyed seeing each other at an Imaginarium convention in Louisville, Kentucky.

Molly MacRae, Author and Lynda Rees, Author. Molly and I met when we both signed books at Prime Crime in Indianapolis.

Awareness is important. You must be visible to the public. You must reach your target readership. Do you need a publicist? That is entirely up to you, depending on how much you know about and enjoy working with social media, libraries, bookstores, bloggers, etc. If you have no clue how to do this or don't want to, there are a lot of great publicists out there.

Your writer organization can be a great source for finding a reliable and effective publicist. Check MWA, SIC or RWA. Most writer organizations post an approved list of marketing agencies and publicists. If yours doesn't, ask your fellow authors for referrals in a forum or on social media. Your peers will be happy to tell you what works for them and what doesn't. That is the beauty of networking.

Be sure of what to expect when working with a vendor. What is their specialty? What do you want? What are you willing to pay for that service? What can you live without?

Before you contract an agency be sure of what you're getting for your money. Establishing clarity about details and expectations up front will pay off in the long run.

There are as many ways of launching and marketing books as there are stars in the sky. Among the most prevalent are:

- Pre-Launch Campaign
- Book Launch – in person, online party, FB takeover, invite only Zoom party, virtual book tour
- Interview - TV/Radio/Online/Newspaper Campaign/Blog
- Word of Mouth
- Social Media
- Your Launch Team or VIP Group of Fans
- Mail Campaign
- Newsletter
- Online Ad
- Contests / Prize Drawing
- Giveaway
- Free First-in-the-Series
- Book Signing

· Trailers
· YouTube Videos
· Swag

What you choose to spend your valuable time and energy on depends on your goals and budget.

I personally have not used a publicist, though I am open to it. I have used my VIP fans, newsletter, social media, author organizations, and online groups I belong to, to get the word out. Having a marketing background this isn't difficult for me but might be for some.

I write my press releases, advertising copy, create my book trailers and load them to my website and YouTube channel.

I reach out to bloggers and set up virtual and in person book tours, book launches and personal appearances.

If you don't know how to do these things or don't want to, you should consider hiring a professional to take this off your shoulders. Of course, this depends on your goals and what you can afford.

BOOK TRAILERS

Most of marketing functions are self-explanatory, and you've probably read many in-depth articles on what they are and how they can benefit sales or exposure of your book. Book trailers are a great tool that is rarely discussed. I believe the subject warrants greater explanation. So, we're going to discuss them a bit here.

A book trailer is similar to a movie trailer. You generally see movie trailers played as television commercials for a film. They are also aired in a theatre prior to the feature film, while they have you in your seat, a captured audience. It's a great time to advertise what is coming soon, so they can draw you back to the big screen time and time again.

You can harness the power of this awesome tactic and use a similar 'come-again' strategy to drive awareness and sales of your books.

How? First, decide what message you want the trailer to convey. Don't tell the story. Tell the watcher who you want to become a reader of the book, what they will experience when they read it. Project the mood, feel, and basic concept in a few slides and audio. Entertain. Make it dramatic or soft and sweet, scary, or wary, whatever the book brings to the picture.

First create a storyboard of what you want to say about your book—not the story but the benefit it brings the reader. Each page should hit some key point you want to drive home to entice the watcher, but not to tell the tail. You want them to purchase the book for that.

Find visuals that represent each storyboard page. Select the font, color scope, and setting aura you want to convey. Choose a tune or audio that represents the mood you want to project. Or write copy and have a narrator create the reading you want to play with the visual. Create a title page, the storyboard pages, the ending message, a page about the author.

Don't forget to end the storyboard with a page of buy links and a strong, short call to action. This is the part many book trailers forget to add. It can be the most important page of the presentation.

Set this presentation into motion and add the audio to it. It's ready to use.

What do I do with it? Post it on your YouTube Channel. If you don't have one, go to the site. There are simple instructions on how to create one.

Post the trailer on your website or post a link to it.

Share the link on all social media formats. Send the link to your tribe and readership. Ask them to SUBSCRIBE to your YouTube Channel, to LIKE the trailer, and to SHARE it with their followers and friends.

Share it with bloggers who host you. Share it to media contacts you send press releases to. Post on FB, Twitter, or wherever you hang out socially. Add it to the back or front matter of your books. . Share it with anyone and anyplace that might provide awareness to the public about your book. There are as many places as you can possibly think of to share your book trailer. The list is endless.

Where can I get help? There are many services available to help you or to create book trailers for you. Or you can learn from one of the services how to create a book trailer for yourself. Here are just a few:

http://www.booktrailerservices.com/

Book Trailer Service | LITERARY TITAN

Affordable Book Trailers! – Writers Weekly Marketplace

Book Trailers Creation Services Company - Video Production Agency (penguinbookwriters.com)

https://canva.com

Hey, catch me on a good day, I might offer my service to create one for you. Don't be shy. It's worth asking. I've done many of them and depending on workload, may be available. https://LyndaReesAuthor.com

PRESS RELEASE

If you live in a tiny burg that is starving for local news, they may be interested in the fact you published a book. If so, feel free to reach out to them with your launch announcement, especially if you are hosting a book launch party at some local business. Be sure to send along photos, a book cover, an author photo, and buy links along with the press release.

If not, then a press release about the launch of your book may not be worth creating. These are exceptions.

- If the book has some hook that plays well in the media.
- The story is about a special news-worthy topic.
- It relates in some way to news of popular interest.
- It relates to some current event.
- It supports a news-worthy cause or charity.

If any of these are the case, go for it. Write a press release. Start with the heading as the date and **FOR IMMEDIATE RELEASE**. Next add a title to the release. The body of the release should include:

- **Who** is making the announcement. That would be you and/or your publisher.
- It should explain:
  - **What** you're announcing

- ○ **When** it's happening
- ○ **Where** it's happening, and
- ○ **Why** they should be interested
- · End with **Contact Information** and **Buy Links**.
- · Embed any visuals you want to share (book cover, author photo, logo, etc.). Also, attach these to the email when you send them to the press. Be sure to include a note in the email letter confirming who owns the visuals you're sending them.

PRESS KIT (See Handout Page for template.)

Your book is published. How do you manage all the details?

A press kit is a must. You cannot wait to create this. As details are established about publication of your book, you need to start putting them into a file.

I use an online file folder called Press Kit for each book and file that folder under the book's folder. This is a one-stop-shop location where I can grab and distribute information required to publicize my book.

For instance, you have an opportunity to be interviewed. Send the press kit to the publisher so they're prepared to create an interesting interview and have what they need to publicize it.

They don't want a folder full of items. They will want a one-page summary with it all listed for them, and they'll want photos of the cover and your headshot. Even if you embed these jpgs into the one-page Press Kit, they may prefer you attach them separately to the mailer when you reach out to them.

You can use the kit to manage advertising, social media, etc., to get the word out to the public about your book. This saves time so you're not constantly looking in several places for specific information about the book.

Should you add books to this series, this Press Kit can be a valuable reference for certain material as you write the next book.

I've provided a template for a one-page Info Sheet you can use in your Press Kit. It's one tool I use when creating a press kit. I fill this form out as details are available. I'm sure you will find it helpful, too.

It includes items such as:

· Author press photo, name, author tag line, BIO, logo

· Book title, photo of book cover, advertising photos, SBN numbers, number pages, number words, retailer buy links, prices, and anything else relevant to the book.

· Publisher information

· Book tag and log lines, blurbs, synopsis

· Reviews and a list and links to author interviews and podcasts

· Link to book website page, author social media links, link to newslette

· Links to book trailers

· Translation information and links

· List of published books by author

You might not have all this information up front. That's okay. Start filling in the form as any related book data is established. Add to it as details become available. It should be a continual work in progress.

HOMEWORK:

1. Write a list of thirty ways you might like to market your books. Don't judge. Just brainstorm.
2. Wait a day. Read the list again. Prioritize the items by numbering them 1-30
3. Develop a plan to tackle the first three.
4. Once you have a plan for those three, tackle the next three. Etc.

REMEMBER THE 4 P SYSTEM

PROACTIVE – PROFESSIONAL –
POSITIVE - PERSISTENT

CHAPTER FIFTEEN
PLATFORM

These days before publishing your works, distributors and agents expect you to have a Platform. That term may be confusing to beginners. A platform is a location where your fans and readers can find you. It's a place where you communicate with them. Let me clarify what they're looking for.

The first thing is an author website. There was a time when a publisher or publicist might help you create or create a website for the author. However, that no longer applies.

WEBSITE

Websites can be expensive to create, or they can be relatively cheap. They can be difficult to create and maintain, or they can be simple. I prefer simplicity myself, as long as it looks professional.

There are many places to build them. I've found for me; WordPress is the easiest to use. There is availability for you to start out with a FREE website. If you are serious about this business, I highly recommend you should seek to own your own URL for your website. Owning your own URL is possible with all of the options out there and most of them for a very small price.

Your website is where you want to drive traffic. So, you can concentrate your efforts elsewhere to send people to your website. Why? Well, it's simple. You want them to have the option to learn about you, your books, to purchase them and to join your team of reader fans.

As you build the site keep equity in mind. You want the appearance of the website to reflect your brand character in look and feel. Check out the websites of some of your favorite, successful authors. What is user friendly? What catches your eye? What functions or type visuals get attention and/or action. Consider mimicking someone successful in the way you design your own site.

What should be on your website?

1. A photo of yourself, some information about you—what you want your fans to know about you.
2. Your logo.
3. A link so fans can follow your blog if you have one.
4. A link so readers can sign up for your fan club and receive your emails.
5. Links to your social media pages.
6. Establish a page for each of your books. Include a cover shot, the blurb, and retailer buy links.
7. If you want buyers to purchase direct, this is where you establish the purchase links your online store.
8. Photos of characters, links to interviews you or a character did for the book.
9. Book reviews.
10. Possibly, fun things that pertain to your writing life, your books, or you personally—things you don't mind sharing.
11. Social media icon widgets with links encouraging readers to share what they see there with their followers and fans on their own social media platforms.

You can hire an expert to build a site for you, or you can build your site or do it yourself. Your writer organization may have training on how to set up a website. It might be worth taking. WordPress has great Help information available on their site and some awesome templates you can choose from. These can be tailored to fit your brand image. Other website platforms do as well.

SOCIAL MEDIA

This is a two-sided blade. Social media is great in one way but awful in another. It can be a brilliant way of cheaply creating awareness. It can also be a massive time-sucker. Try not to go down that spiraling well.

That said, social media has become integral to our daily lives. There are 4.8 billion social media users worldwide. This accounts for 59+% of the world's population. We rely on these outlets as ways of staying in touch with friends and relatives, for research and gathering information, and to build and grow our businesses, regardless of what they are. *(Data courtesy of SearchEngineJournal.cm)*. Because of social media networks, we have grown to expect real-time news and updates and have learned to trust what we find there. This should not always be the case, but it's a reality. This makes being involved in social media an expected part of doing business.

There are many social media outlets out there. So many, in fact, that it's impossible to be active on every one of them every day. The key is to **choose the right platform** for your brand. Where do your readers hang out during their spare time? Where are they searching for books or advice on books? In essence, where is your target audience spending their time? That's where it makes sense for you to become active.

Establish a pattern and method of reaching them on those platforms on a continual basis. When? With What? How often? Well, that depends on the social media platform. TikTok and Twitter are fast-rolling blasts of media. You might need to post to them 3-4 times a day. These can be scheduled but need to be frequent. Others, like Facebook or YouTube, may not require as frequent posts.

Below is a list of the most common social media platforms. There are new ones coming along constantly. Choose the ones that will get you the biggest fan buck for your time. Establish a **Professional Page** presence on those social media sites and decide how often and what type of content you will use to reach your target audience.

Even within these, there are special ways to reach your audience. For instance, in Facebook there are specific Groups you can join that want to hear about books, authors, writing and/or reading. Likewise, there are Groups looking for information on many specific subjects.

You might want to Follow or Like authors who write books similar to yours. They will likely Like and/or Follow you back. Either way, you will be able to reach their fan base as well as yours. By Commenting, Sharing, Liking or Reposting other's work, you are linking with them. It's a scratch your back, I'll scratch yours benefit.

What do you post? Eash venue is different and has unique aspects, benefits, tools, and expectations. It is a good idea to set up your page and begin to watch what others do. Like and Follow other authors who write in your genre. See what they do. If you see high levels of activity happening around their offerings, they are doing something well. You may want to consider emulating them.

Your readership wants to know about your books, other books, about you personally (what you choose to share with them), and they want to be entertained. Don't make it all about 'buy my book.' Make it engaging and entertaining.

Here are some social media platforms.

- Facebook
- Twitter
- Pinterest
- YouTube
- Instagram
- TikTok
- BookTok
- SnapChat

· FaceBook

REMEMBER THE 4 P SYSTEM

PROACTIVE – PROFESSIONAL – POSITIVE - PERSISTENT

CHAPTER SIXTEEN

BUSINESS DOS AND DON'TS

- Whether self-set or by a publisher, agent, editor, or other vendor you are working with, be professional.
- Meet deadlines.
- Be cordial and respectful.
- Don't expect your agent, editor, or other vendor you work with to be available 24/7. They have lives too, and you're not their only author. Their time is valuable. Use it wisely.
- Be reasonable. These people are not there to do you harm. They are there to help you.
- Know your genre and subgenre. Be sure your book is categorized correctly.
- Key words are the key to getting your book noticed.
- Do clarify expectations up front, no matter who you are working with.
- Don't sign a contract without understanding fully what rights you are signing away. (Audio, translation, movie or film rights, gaming, televised syndication, etc.) If you

don't agree with the term, ask in a professional manner to have them changed before signing. If they disagree, rethink your position. If it's important to you, you may wish to walk away from a contract where valuable rights are being tied up and maybe never used.

· Understand how long rights are held and the process should you decide to withdraw them from the contract, should the publisher stop working on your book after a specified period.

· Understand what happens to your rights, should the publisher go out of business.

· Determine whether to go exclusive with an indie-publisher or go wide. This is an individual choice, depending on your goals and preference.

· It's a good idea to have an entertainment attorney review a contract before signing.

· It's a good idea to have a professional tax expert manage your taxes.

· The huge learning curve for beginning Indie-published authors is steep, but once you've published a couple books, you'll flow through the complex process easily.

PROFESSIONAL HELP / RESOURCES

Your best resource can be your professional writer organization and your peers. Find your tribe and use their expertise. Don't forget to give back as you learn, to share with other up-and-coming writers. Below are a few resources I've used. I hope you find them helpful.

- The Emotion Thesaurus, A Writer's Guide to Character Expression by Angela Ackerman & Becca Puglist is a help guide I find indispensable. I keep it beside my computer and refer to it continually. It's my favorite reference book.
- Buy a good thesaurus and a hard copy dictionary. Keep them handy.
- Chicago Manual Of Style Online https://www.chicago-manualofstyle.org
- The Writer's Almanac http://writersalmanac.org
- Grammar Girl http://www.quickanddirtytips.com/grammar-girl
- Write Globe: https://writeglobe.com/
- Urban Dictionary https://www.urandictionary.com
- Marie Force's Formatting Faries https://www.Marie-Force.com/Fairies/
- Merry Banerji / Meredith Bond, Anessa Books, Formatting and Coachingwww.anessabooks.com and merrybond.books@gmail.com
- IngramSpark https://myaccount.ingramspark.com/
- FindawayVoices / Spotify (produce/publish audiobooks) https://findawayvoices.com/
- Scrivener | Literature & Latte https://www.literature-andlatte.com
- Grammarly (Self-Editing Resource—Note: This is fine for getting the manuscript ready for submission to your editor. I do not recommend solely self-editing). Offers Free Proofreading Tool and Tips: https://grammerly.com

There are some useful resources at this link on my website. Check them out.

FOR AUTHORS – Lynda Rees, Author, The Murder Guru (https://www.lyndareesauthor.com)

WRAP UP

Thank you for reading *It's YOUR Business, For Authors and Creative Businessowners.* I love reading helpful books and taking classes to hone my craft and stay in tune with changes in the industry. I have found that no matter the subject there's always at least one valuable thing I learn that I can execute to make my business run smother and better. That is what I hope for you with this book.

I've enjoyed spending this time with you and hope we become great friends. Please, join my VIP group and reach out to me anytime. I'm always happy to help fellow authors. Please stay in touch.

Have a blessed year and a profitable writing venture.

Sincerely,

Lynda Rees, The Murder Guru

Love is a dangerous mystery. Enjoy the ride!©

Become a VIP https://preview.mailerlite.com/t1a6j6

Website: www.lyndareesauthor.com

Email: www.lyndareesauthor@gmail.com

GOLDEN HEART AWARD, RITA & IMAGINARIUM FINAL-IST

YouTube Channel   https://bit.ly/2HmSA9M

AllAuthor   https://allauthor.com/author/lyndarees/

Bookbub https://www.bookbub.com/profile/lynda-rees

Goodreads   https://www.goodreads.com/author/show/17187400.Lynda_Rees

Twitter https://twitter.com/LyndaReesauthor

Facebook: https://www.facebook.com/lynda.rees.author/

Instagram @lyndareesauthor.com

Pinterest https://www.pinterest.com/lyndareesauthor/pins/

REMEMBER THE 4 P SYSTEM

PROACTIVE – PROFESSIONAL – POSITIVE - PERSISTENT

CHAPTER SEVENTEEN
HANDOUTS:
Action Plan

Link: https://dl.bookfunnel.com/pfsqvz0ggp

GOAL	STRATEGY	TACTIC	MEASURE
1	A.	A.1 A.2 A.3	
	B.	B.1 B.2 B.3	
	C.	C.1 C.2 C.3	
2	A.	A.1 A.2 A.3	
	B.	B.1 B.2 B.3	
	C.	C.1 C.2 C.3	
3	A.	A.1 A.2	
	B.	B.1 B.2	
	C.	C.1 C.2	
4	A.	A.1 A.2	
	B.	B.1 B.2	
	C.	C.1 C.2	

HANDOUT:
Book INFO Template
Link: https://dl.bookfunnel.com/owza3qhgkm

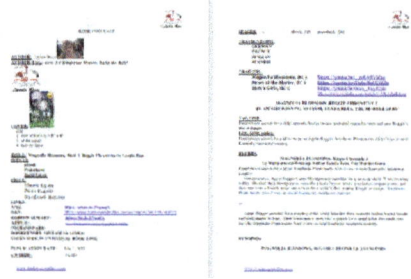

HANDOUTS:
Launch Plan
Link: https://dl.bookfunnel.com/90eb6zpun9

HANDOUTS:

Bookmarks

Link: https://dl.bookfunnel.com/eu8nzxukkp

HANDOUTS:
Budget Spreadsheet Template
Link: https://dl.bookfunnel.com/a0dye9czhi

HANDOUTS:
Business Plan Template
Link: https://dl.bookfunnel.com/jb27aq23b7

HANDOUTS:
Business Plan Example (Lynda Rees)
Link: https://dl.bookfunnel.com/d3kywmmwvk

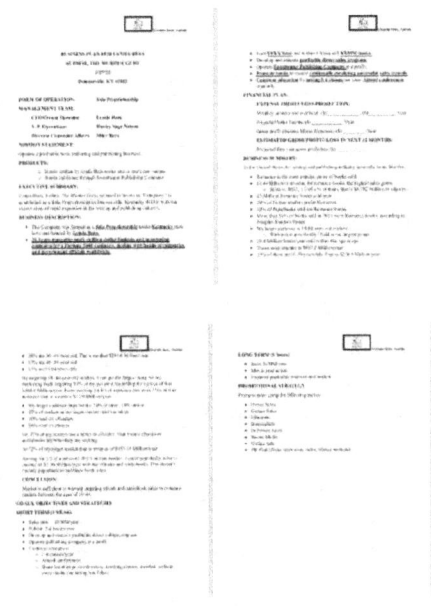

HANDOUTS:

Character Development

Link: https://dl.bookfunnel.com/fndpk9htjo

BOOK DIARY   CHARACTER DEVELOPMENT

NAME	ROLE	NOTES
Hair		
Eyes		
Height		
Distinctive Appearance		
Job		
Past Business Experience		
Relationship Status		
Previous Relationship(s)		
Key Skills/Talents		
Pr[?]/Dream Role		
Likes		
Dislikes		
Fears		
Dreams/Aspirations		
Unattainable Desires		
Internal Conflict		
External Conflict		
Motivation		
Personality-What makes him distinctive?		
Fatal Flaw		
Best Friend(s)		
Worst Enemies		
Location of Birth		
Grew Up Where?		
Lives Where?		
Plans		
What's At Risk?		
He/She Cares For/Protects		
He/She Hiding		
Why Desire is Unattainable		
Quirks/Flaws/Scars/Habits		
Music Preference/Dislikes		
Food Likes/Dislikes		
He/She's Running From		
He/She's Settling For		
Family		
Boss/Relationship With Boss		
Co-Workers		
How Co-Workers & Friends See Him/Her?		

138

HANDOUTS:
Creative Brief

Link: https://dl.bookfunnel.com/lcm3m4px5r

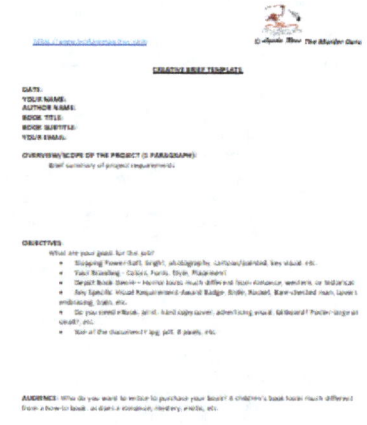

HANDOUTS:

Business Dos and Don'ts

Link: https://dl.bookfunnel.com/yognm9856z

BUSINESS DOS AND DON'TS

• Whether self-set or by a publisher, agent, editor or other vendor you are working with, be professional.

• Meet deadlines.

• Be cordial and respectful.

• Don't expect your agent, editor or other vendor you work with to be available 24/7. They have lives too, and you're not their only author. Their time is valuable. Use it wisely.

• Be reasonable. These people are not there to do your bidding. They are there to help you.

• Know your genre and subgenre. Be sure your book is categorized correctly. Key words are the key to getting your book noticed.

• Do clarify expectations up front, no matter who you are working with.

• Don't sign a contract without understanding fully what rights you are signing away. (Audio, translations, movie or film rights, gaming, televised syndication, etc.) If you don't agree with the term, ask in a professional manner to have them changed before signing. If they disagree, rethink your position. If it's important to you, you may wish to walk away from a contract where valuable rights are being tied up and maybe never used.

• Understand how long rights are held and the process should you decide to withdraw them from a contract, should the publisher stop working on your book after a specified period.

• Understand what happens to your rights, should the publisher go out of business.

• Determine whether to go exclusive with an indie-publisher or go wide. This is an individual choice, depending on your goals and preference.

• It's a good idea to have an entertainment attorney review a contract before signing.

• It's a good idea to have a professional tax expert manage your taxes.

• The huge learning curve for beginning Indie published authors is steep, but once you've published a couple books, you'll flow through the complex process easily.

www.lyndazcreations.com

HANDOUTS:
File Sample
Link: https://dl.bookfunnel.com/m1572xyouk

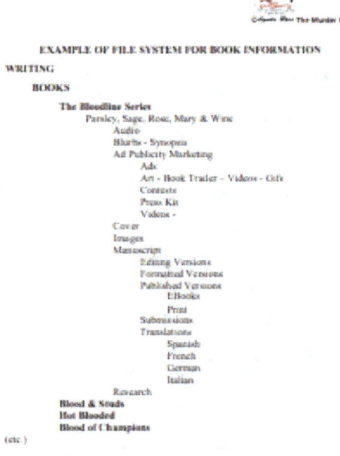

HANDOUTS:

MRI Violation

Link: https://dl.bookfunnel.com/oiofhz5zhr

Motivation Reaction Unit

A well-done MRU pulls your reader further into your story, so there's tons of hype about it. It's a big deal. We want that, right?

Scenes roll out in a series of causes and effects or a series of motivations and reactions. We string enough motivations and reactions together, and we've created a compelling scene.

So what is an MRU? What are the elements making up an MRU?
1. Motivation: A stimulus occurring outside the character.
2. Character: Reaction happening inside the character.

Example of an MRU: The ice melted as he touched it. (This shows motivation stimulus—happening outside the character.) He jerked his finger back and dumped the ice. (This shows the character's reaction.)

Note: The character is NEVER the subject of the motivating stimulus.

Never say: He felt the blade against his skin. Nix the "he felt". It takes the story out of his POV. It tells vs. showing, and it distances readers—a No-No.

Let's break down the character reaction, as part of the MRU.

3 Parts of Reaction:

1. Visceral: Emotional response that immediately overtakes your character. He or she has no control over this response. This is the first response.
2. Reflex: Action kicks in. What does he physically do? Does he jerk? Twitch? Scream? Run? Cry?
3. Rational Action (not a reflex) and/or Speech: After his immediate emotional response and instinctive action, your character does or says something he or she has control over—something thought out vs. instinctive.

Important note: **This must be in order.** Motivating stimulus must come first. Your character can't react to something that hasn't happened. It doesn't happen simultaneously, but in order.

Don't write: She screamed and jerked her finger to her mouth **after** the blade sliced her skin. This reads incorrectly—the MRU is out of order and backwards.

Components **must** stay in order. Motivation must occur outside the character to bring on an intuitive reaction. This emotional reaction **always** precedes physical action or speech. Scalding water splashes flesh and engages nerve endings as they burn. Then you scream and shove your finger in your mouth. **Not** the other way around.

Get the order right and hook your reader.

Get the order wrong, your reader realizes something is strange. They may not be able to verbalize it or know what it is, but they are aware something is incorrect.

HANDOUTS:
Promo Code Tracker
Link: https://dl.bookfunnel.com/ksy7niajm1

HANDOUTS:

Resources

Link: https://dl.bookfunnel.com/t42zmjsay1

PROFESSIONAL HELP / RESOURCES

Your best resource can be your professional writer organization and your peers. Find your tribe and use their expertise. Don't forget to give back as you learn, to share with other up-and-coming writers. Below are a few resources I've used. I hope you find them helpful.

- The Emotion Thesaurus, A Writer's Guide to Character Expression by Angela Ackerman & Becca Puglisi is a help guide I find indispensable. I keep it beside my computer and refer to it continually. It's my favorite reference book.
- Buy a good thesaurus and a hard copy dictionary. Keep them handy.
- Chicago Manual Of Style Online https://www.chicagomanualofstyle.org
- The Writer's Almanac http://writersalmanac.org
- Grammar Girl https://www.quickanddirtytips.com/grammar-girl
- Write Globe: https://writeglobe.com/
- Urban Dictionary https://www.urbandictionary.com
- Marie Forae's Formatting Forces https://www.MarieForae.com/formatting
- Merry Banerji / Meredith Bond. Anessa Books, Formatting and Coaching www.anessabooks.com and merrybond.books@gmail.com
- IngramSpark https://www.ingramspark.com
- Findaway Voices (produce/publish audiobooks) https://findawayvoices.com
- Scrivener Scrivener | Literature & Latte (literatureandlatte.com)
- Grammarly (Self-Editing Resource—Note: This is fine for getting the manuscript ready for submission to your editor. I do not recommend solely self-editing) (app.grammarly.com) and (us.grammarly.com)

- Meredith Bond & Pru Warren https://thewritersblockpartypodcast.com
- Lisa Cron, Wired for Story http://amazon.to/2exemm6
- Lisa Cron, Story Genius https://amzn.to/30o6itz
- Stephen King, On Writing https://amzn.to/2tuhbin
- Larry Brooks, Story Engineering https://amzn.to/3infuzm
- Debra Dixon, Goal, Motivation, and Conflict https://amzn.to/2xu9mo
- Alicia Rasley, The Power of Point of View https://amzn.to/30us6sf
- Bob Mayer, Novel Writer's Toolbox, https://amzn.to/2jeuqwu
- Renni Browne & Dave King, Self-Editing For Fiction Writers https://amzn.to/2xl7gaw

There are some useful resources at this link on my website. Check them out. FOR AUTHORS – **Lynda Rees, Author, The Murder Guru** (https://www.lyndareesauthor.com) at https://lyndareesauthor.com/2021/06/05/2036.

HANDOUTS:

Submission Tracker Template

Link: https://dl.bookfunnel.com/yyt5rxaepd

HANDOUTS:
Writer Organizations
Link: https://dl.bookfunnel.com/4kzb47x7rg

WRITER ORGANIZATIONS

There are many more, some dedicated to specific genres. These are only a few I have personal experience with. They provide outlets for networking, essential resources, critical information, training, and a means to meet movers and shakers in the industry and like-minded writers. I find them essential to a professional author.

RWA – ROMANCE WRITERS OF AMERICA https://rwa.org

MWA – MYSTERY WRITERS OF AMERICA https://mwa@mysterywriters.org

CWA – CRIME WRITERS OF AMERICA https://contemporaryromans.e.org

SiC – SISTERS IN CRIME https://sistersincrime.org

CRW – CONTEMPORARY ROMANCE WRITERS https://contemporaryromance.org

BCW – BUCKEYE CRIME WRITERS https://buckeyecrimewriters.org

GLFW – GREAT LAKES FICTION WRITERS P.O. Box 360980, Strongsville, OH 44136 greatlakesfictionw@gmail.com

KRW – KENTUCKIANA ROMANCE WRITERS https://groups.google.com/d/forum/writersromance

KH - KENTUCKY HUMANITIES https://kyhumanities.org

LITERARY CLEVELAND (HUMANITIES) https://litcleveland.org

NOTE: Lynda Rees does not personally endorse any organization.

HANDOUTS:

Goal Setting Tool

Link: https://dl.bookfunnel.com/8e4zdse8b6

HANDOUTS:

SWAG Vendors

Link: https://dl.bookfunnel.com/e9w79piu6c

SWAG VENDORS

There are many vendors who can create personalized swag items. Swag is valuable to your business. It helps remind a reader they met you, after the first impression. It can be anything from shirts, coffee cups, drink coaster, mouse pads, hats, totes, to bookmarks or business cards. The key to SWAG is to include your **website address** and/or **buy links**, an invite for them to join your **Fan Club** and your **logo** or at least your **name**. My favorite vendors.

John Lurking at Proforma Albrechter Company (Almost anything you can think of. Offers bulk discounts, so ask John for that vs. the catalogue price. Tell him I sent you.)
515-673-6000 john@luckingonline.com

VistaPrint (Paper products , stickers, business cards, book marks, apparel, luggage, mugs, etc.) https://VistaPrint.com

Banners.com (Any type banner or poster) https://banners.com

National Pen (Pens, day planners, calendars, and more)
https://NationalPen.com

Pens.Com (Pens and other misc. gifts) https://Pens.com

Country Patchwork, (858) 351-1118 (Personalized mugs, insulated drink vessels and many other things. You name it. They can help.)
countrypatchworld@gmail.com
Cindy Wade, Kim Bailey, Karen Davis Kdavis1670@yahoo.com

Decals.com (anything sticker or decal)
https://connectjodecals.com, 320-391-5250

Incredible Cookies (Book cover personalized cookies)
https://Incrediblecookies.com

Callie (personalized jewelry, etc.)
https://Callie.com

HANDOUTS:
Edit Out Words and Phrases
Link: https://dl.bookfunnel.com/q5x6tlt29l

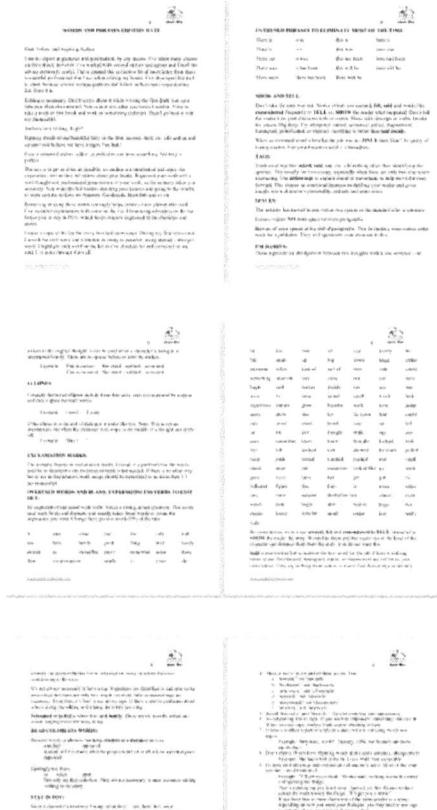

HANDOUTS (Links only)

Below are links so you can download templates and hand-outs mentioned in this book. If you would like any of these handouts in magnet-back or laminated format, reach out to me. They are available for $5 each.

Action Plan Link: https://dl.bookfunnel.com/pfsqvz0ggp

Book INFO Template Link: https://dl.bookfunnel.com/owza3qhgkm

Launch Plan Link: https://dl.bookfunnel.com/90eb6zpun9

Bookmarks Link: https://dl.bookfunnel.com/eu8nzxukkp

Budget Spreadsheet Template Link: https://dl.bookfunnel.com/a0dye9czhi

Business Plan Template Link: https://dl.bookfunnel.com/jb27aq23b7

Business Plan Example (Lynda Rees) Link: https://dl.bookfunnel.com/d3kywmmwvk

Character Development Link: https://dl.bookfunnel.com/fndpk9htjo

Creative Brief Link: https://dl.bookfunnel.com/lcm3m4px5r

Business Dos and Don'ts Link: https://dl.bookfunnel.com/yognm9856z

File Sample Link: https://dl.bookfunnel.com/m1572xyouk

MRI Violation Link: https://dl.bookfunnel.com/oiofhz5zhr

Promo Code Tracker Link: https://dl.bookfunnel.com/ksy7niajm1

Resources Link: https://dl.bookfunnel.com/t42zmjsay1

Submission Tracker Template Link: https://dl.bookfunnel.com/yyt5rxaepd

Writer Organizations Link: https://dl.bookfunnel.com/4kzb47x7rg

Goal Setting Tool Link: https://dl.bookfunnel.com/8e4zdse8b6

SWAG Vendors Link: https://dl.bookfunnel.com/e9w79piu6c

EDIT OUT WORDS AND PHRASES Link: https://dl.bookfunnel.com/q5x6tlt29l

NOTE:

If you need any of these spreadsheets in EXCEL or CSV format, reach out to the author at lyndareesauthor@gmail.com.

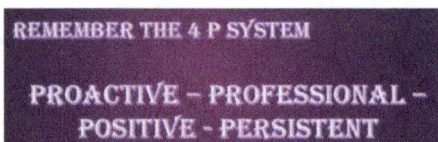

REMEMBER THE 4 P SYSTEM

PROACTIVE – PROFESSIONAL –
POSITIVE - PERSISTENT

BOOKS BY LYNDA REES

Love is a dangerous mystery.
Enjoy the ride!

Linda Rees

HISTORICAL ROMANCE:

Gold Lust Conspiracy

MYSTERY:

Fresh Starts, Dirty Money
Flip or Flop, Murder House
God Father's Day
Madam Mom
2nd Chance Ranch
Operation Second Chance
The Bloodline Series:
Leah's Story
Parsley, Sage, Rose, Mary & Wine
Blood & Stud
Hot Blooded
Blood of Champions
Bloodlines & Lies
Horseshoes & Roses
The Bloodline Trail
Real Money

The Bourbon Trail
Reggie Chronicles:
Hart's Girls
Heart of the Matter
Magnolia Blossoms
CHILDREN'S MIDDLE-GRADE MYSTERY:
Freckle Face & Blondie
The Thinking Tree
CHILDREN'S PICTURE AND ACTIVITY BOOKS:
NO FEAR
NO FEAR Learning and Activity Book
NON-FICTION:
EASY KETO GUIDE
EASY KETO
EASY KETO Cooking
EASY KETO Desserts
EASY KETO Journal
EASY KETO 7 Day Meal Planner *
EASY KETO Shopping List *
EASY KETO Cheatsheet *

*Available in Laminated or Magnet-Back Format upon email request.

Find information about these books at website: https://www.lyndareesauthor.com

Book trailers at YouTube Channel: https://bit.ly/2HmSA9M